APERTURE

ON LOCATION: Studio Visits with

ON LOCATION

Lynn Davis

The work presented in *Aperture*'s third "On Location" issue reveals that we live in a constant state of transformation, that the naming of things does not make them any more tangible, that the "decisive moment" is over before it begins, and that the "fixative" nature of photography makes it marvelously complicit in its paradoxical relationship with the world.

These dynamics, however, do not undermine the power of photography. As seen here in the work of Lynn Davis, Mary Ellen Mark, Duane Michals, Richard Misrach, Raghu Rai, Lise Sarfati, and Doug and Mike Starn, they may inspire images that are profoundly experiential and filled with possibilities that transcend the singular moment.

The sublime evocation of metamorphoses in Lynn Davis's work—where nudes may resemble both the man-made and the natural landscape, and vice versa, where that which is solid feels fluid, and where "negative" space gives the illusion of mass—echoes her own sense of the mutability of things. Also offering a nonlinear take on time and space, where mutability is the only constant, are Doug and Mike Starn. As comfortable working with NASA as in SoHo, these identical twins fuse art, science, and the spiritual, while layering images, text, and now even live bugs, in consideration of the ephemeral nature of art itself.

Doug and Mike Starn

As India celebrates its fiftieth year of independence, the Indian photographer Raghu Rai presents a country in perpetual transition, where the ancient and the contemporary sometimes clash, and where various delineations—borders, classes, religious and political beliefs—are continually evolving. Meanwhile, the epic proportions of Russia's current transitional period, symbolically evoked by the French photographer Lise Sarfati in her project "The Memory and the Flight," are conveyed in a particularly intimate and human way through her story of two transsexuals. Here, the idea of transformation is poignantly elucidated in Sarfati's description of Aza and Alexandra, and their desire to alter their very beings.

Raghu Rai (center)

Lise Sarfati (right)

Also respecting the integrity of each individual while creating metaphorical images is Mary Ellen Mark. Her portraits of teenagers—an age group on which she has often focused—seem extraordinarily intuitive, manifesting essential qualities of her subjects' identities during this precariously pivotal period in their lives. Mark's portfolio includes figures who have featured prominently in her work over the years: Tiny, from *Streetwise*, and Chrissy and Jesse Damm—all of whom, in a sense, Mark has watched grow up. Duane Michals focuses on coming into one's own in a very introspective way. From the allegory of the prodigal son to ideals of youth, the evolution of sexual desire, and ultimately the sense of self, Michals's work is infused with an almost melancholic awareness of aging and the ego. This, coupled with his often whimsical style, reiterates the inevitability of time passing, the underlying theme in so much of Michals's photography.

Mary Ellen Mark

Duane Michals

Richard Misrach's in-progress, never-before-published twenty-first "Desert Canto," comprised of night skies, also suggests moments of passage, but perhaps of a more cyclical nature. By virtue of the long exposure of his camera, Misrach's "Heavenly Bodies [sic]," animated by an unfathomable choreography of stars, reveals the heavens's continual metamorphoses—"'Scuse me while I kiss the sky!" (OK—so Jimi Hendrix comes to mind before Alfred Stieglitz or Edward Abbey.)

The inherent sense of impermanence in the images presented in this issue broadens the time-arresting notion of photography. Davis, Mark, Michals, Misrach, Rai, Sarfati, and the Starns offer diverse explorations not only into the transformative nature of their own artistic processes but also into the elemental processes of transformation intrinsic to everyday life. As always, *Aperture* appreciates their openness and their generous collaboration.

—THE EDITORS

Richard Misrach

Lynn Davis, *Iceberg #22*, Disko Bay, Greenland, 1988

LYNN DAVIS

INTERVIEW BY MELISSA HARRIS

MELISSA HARRIS: You seem to play with inversions in your work, between mass and void, positive and negative space. Is the negative space as present, as real as the positive space, or is the positive space as illusory as the negative space?
LYNN DAVIS: Many years ago, when I started doing the nudes, I noticed that I seemed to find the perfect picture for myself when I would form the subject, and then look at it, and the positive would disappear. In a way, I could almost look at the photographs from every direction. And it started to teach me about my own sense of looking.

Then when I went from the nude into the environment—after all that training working with dancers, yogis, whatever, in a very tight studio space where there was this refined sense of the positive-negative—I had to find an approach. When I'm at a site, what I do is circle, sort of like an animal would, you know—because I never know exactly from where I'm going to shoot. A lot of times I study the sites from pictures first, and I can actually almost locate myself halfway around the world, standing in a spot. Then I go there, and of course, then you have the elements of the excitement of the place, the energy of the place, the light of the place—and so I have to take all that in. But basically, I circle and circle, and look and look, and arrange things, and then I let it all go. Essentially, the solid part disappears, and it's all about the balance and the positive-negative space. In a sense, then, it becomes nothing. It doesn't matter if it's a pyramid or a person or a mountain, because it all vanishes. And it's that moment in the process I equate almost to—not to say that the photograph will seem good to anybody else—but for me it's like a line of poetry. It's just there. There's no more, there's no less. . . .
MH: And then, when you start thinking about the scale of the image and how you're going to tone it, is that an elaboration on that moment, or is that about something else?
LD: That's an interesting layering process. The sense of tone is where I'd say maybe the most feminine aspect comes in. And I mean that in sort of a strange sense, because certainly men have that, too. But some emotional quality of what it felt like, what the color felt like to me in a place—which doesn't necessarily have anything to do with how it looks. So that emotional equivalent. . . . Often I'll bring back some earth from a place, or other things. With these colors in mind, the printer, Steve Rifkin, and I work intensely to find the tones for each new body of work. We experiment a lot. This part of the process is very collaborative.

The scale is a process of bringing the image to life, and the images usually seem to tell me what size they need to be. As for the actual sense of scale of the place, a lot of times I obliterate it. Or sometimes I leave little keys, you know, like a little person, a little car, the telephone pole, whatever. I often don't really sense the size of a site until I'm there.

Lynn Davis, *Wave Rock*, Hyden, Western Australia, 1991

MH: Because you need to feel it in relation to your own body?
LD: It's the body, but it's also what the site is giving me. I'm somebody who over the years has disappeared more and more, in that my conscious mind has planned everything, but then once I'm actually out and ready to photograph, I kind of let the whole experience take over. What's interesting are the surprises, and what hits me at a gut level or a heart level. Really it's a perception that I'm translating. I'm informing you from all my experience that I've had up to that moment. And if I can translate that, then I've done what I've set out to do.
MH: So it's an accumulative process with an experiential result?
LD: Yes, and the ante gets higher each time, because once you've done a lot of things, you have to go the next step, so to go to the next step you have to go further into yourself. And for me, that's

(continued on page 8)

. . . after walking around the statues and chedis,almost all of which have collapsed, I find a position in front of a "walking" Buddha, a figure that I had never seen before and whose fluid and flowing attitude of "becoming" is not, in fact, found in many other periods. This one is positioned on a raised stone platform, its left hand raised in the "attitude of teaching," the thumb and forefinger delicately joined, the right leg stepping forward, the left heel bent in the process.

But it is the elegance of the slightly curving right hand that holds me. Open and yet hesitant, vulnerable and at the same time reflecting the courage of "walking on," the totally relaxed fingers are androgynous,beyond gender, neither coming nor going, but endlessly becoming. Even so, the fingers seem to beckon. They are slightly seductive, tantalizing, inviting. There is none of the stern detachment of Indian or even Tibetan Buddhist sculpture. I look up at the face, at the erect, confident posture of the body. The whole expression, from the delicately turning fingers to the mysterious beatific smile, is one of total equanimity. The figure walks forward as within an illuminated dream. The journey is not revealed, because it cannot be told and cannot appear. It is a "flight through the air" of one who no longer needs to move at all in order to be anywhere.

Lynn Davis, *Walking Buddha*, Sukhothai, Thailand, 1993

The movement seems beyond grace. Its aesthetic demands contemplation, a focus that suddenly fills me with shock. The Buddha seems to be walking right through me. It is a levitation that is more than I can assimilate. . . .

—RUDOLPH WURLITZER
from *Hard Travel to Sacred Places*

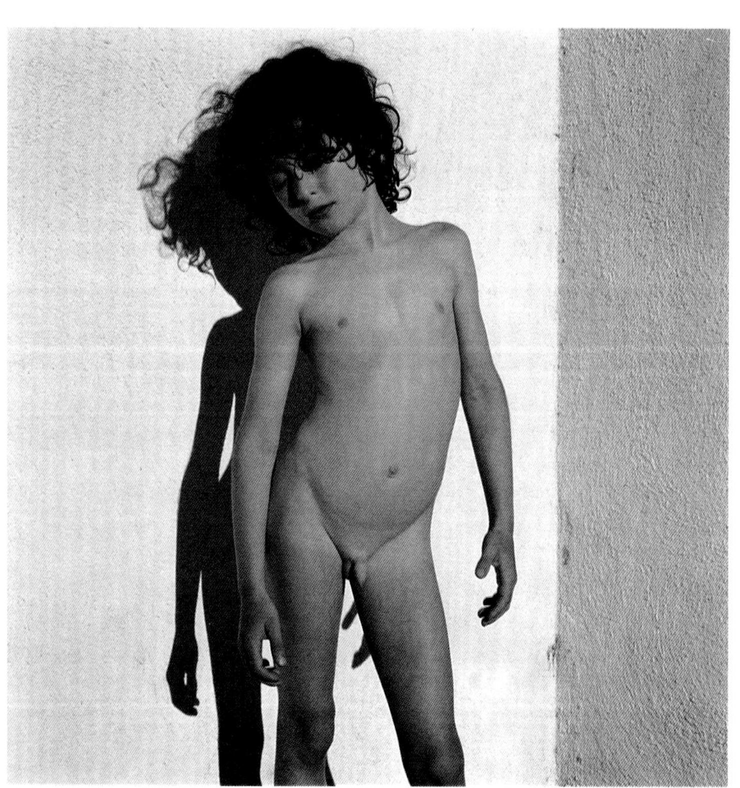

Lynn Davis, *Ayrev Davis*, Los Angeles, 1978

I've fallen in love with the slowness of time,
stillness and perceptions dancing. Makes me
happy, the space and the thought. This ritual,
it's like putting on the brakes. Stop, breathe, and
feel. My meditation, my mantra.

Still, slow and empty
Inhale
Mmmm that's it
Inhale your day

—AYREV DAVIS

Lynn Davis, *Robert Levithan*, New York City, 1978

Lynn Davis, *Dancer*, New York City, 1978

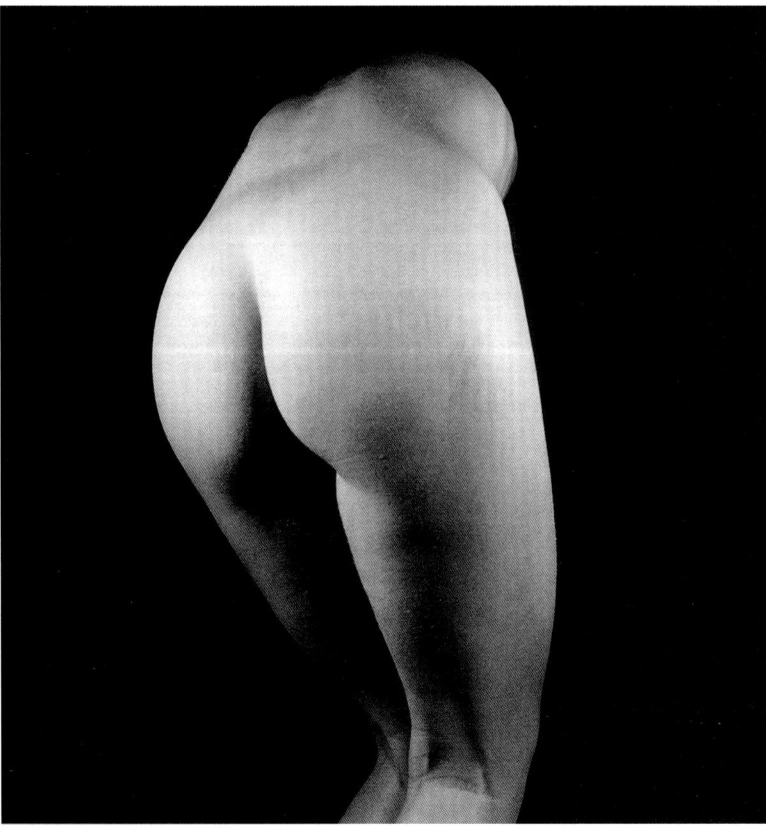

Lynn Davis, *Darlene Banderhoop*, New York City, 1979

(continued from page 5)

letting go a little bit more of the conscious self, and going into the things that maybe are more difficult. I want to produce something that goes a little beyond what I did before, to take some risks personally in order to explore something new.

MH: Can you always recognize your challenges?

LD: I discover them—whether it's trying to get rid of things that are hindrances toward more freedom in the sense of finding a release from one's own neurotic self, or something else. What feeds me now is the lightening up, the lessening of the conscious self toward the more intuitive flowing self. Of course, these are ideas very separate from the pictures. But being that we're talking about process, this is the kind of thing that informs my work. It all starts from inside rather than outside.

MH: What about time? I don't really perceive time in a linear sense in your work, yet there is nothing stagnant about it.

LD: Well, the strange thing here is that ever since the loss of a lot of very important people in my life, time stopped moving forward. I don't know; the next year doesn't seem like it's in front of me, but it's more like a crab moving sideways. Yet one of the things I have really gotten interested in during the last few years is the whole ancient world, and how close I feel to it—which is another total surprise to me. Most of my happiest moments, other than with my husband, Rudy, and the rest of my family and good friends, are out in these spots in the middle of nowhere. I feel completely peaceful, comfortable. And I think that's part of the mystery of my search, what keeps me going to all these places. It isn't about just getting another good picture, although that's part of it. But it's kind of like a great treasure hunt to find something that's inside of you, some kind of peace, some kind of feeling. And I don't think it's about identification. Sometimes I think there is a piece of every great culture in all of us, but you often have to go there and immerse yourself in it in some way to understand something about it. It all goes in, and suddenly, a little piece of me balloons out, and feels like it's developing, or it wasn't there before. And also what drives me is a basic search for this geometry of the circle, square, and triangle as it has evolved and been manifested since the beginning of architecture, throughout every great culture that the world has produced. I love the sense of structure, I love the sense of form, and I love these great sites which were chosen by, well, who knows? Architects? People who had such a feeling for the landscape, and light, and how the buildings would fit, whether they be sacred sites or just great architecture.

What I'm doing is a natural progression of a trip I set out on ten years ago, when I went to Greenland. In this kind of adventure into the unknown, you're really just on the journey of your own life. But you step outside all your own parameters, what you think is right, what you think you're doing.

MH: So you try to get beyond your own preconceptions.

LD: Exactly. Beyond yourself. And let life's journey take over, without your planning and thinking you're in control of everything.

MH: At the time, were you so conscious of this journey?

Lynn Davis, *Giza III, Dynasty IV*, 1989

Lynn Davis, *The Gates of Angkor Thom*, Angkor Wat, Cambodia, 1993

LD: I'd say that the idea of a journey as something with a beginning, middle, and end has been very much in my consciousness since I was, like, twelve years old. So I have always tried to make some sense of events in this way—what can I learn from them?—even though there's often no sense to make. The journey became the thing: not so much Lynn.

MH: Do you try even to make sense of the terribly tragic things that happen in life, such as the accidental death of your twenty-one-year-old son?

LD: In a way, the language is wrong. There is no making sense of it. What there is, is experiencing it. And to do that, you have to just, you know, let it happen. If death starts to happen to people close to you, you start to go on, say, a larger journey. . . . You join all the other people who this has happened to, which is, of course, all the other people in the history of the world.

So I'd say that death has informed me in the sense that I have been living with it and there's no escaping it, but there isn't really a language for it in the sense that you can categorize what happened. All I can say is that it's in everything that I do, it's in how I try to look at relationships, friendships, it's in the conversation that we're having now. I try . . . I don't even try. It's there informing everything now. Especially, of course, when it was my son, Ayrev, who was so deeply, completely part of everything that I did, that you don't even realize how complete until something like that happens to you and they're not there. And if you don't give in to these things—which, believe me, I have no judgments against people who do, because at the end there's something maybe just in your nature that pulls you through, because it is not will—you go on, but in a different way.

Of course, these things are very separate. You could look at my work and never see any of this. But this is all part of my process.

MH: I'm not trying to see your work in terms of this at all.

LD: Yes, but it informs it. And when I'm in these places and things fall together, there is a moment of peace that comes out of it for me personally. In a sense, the specifics of the place don't matter. What I'd like to come across in the work is a presence. A presence where I'm not saying, "Look at this," but rather, where someone looking at the work can become part of it, and sense its nature.

Another subject that interests me is that things are built, and then they reach their peak, and then they fall away, just like you will and just like I will—as will the world. I think that's very exciting . . .

MH: . . . the mutability or impermanence of things?

LD: Yes. And what's getting harder for me to photograph, oddly enough, is solid things.

After my son died, for about two years I became slightly invisible. I couldn't believe anybody could actually see me. I felt like just an accumulation of molecules, only that there were spaces in them so large, anybody could see through them.

MH: Was that frightening?

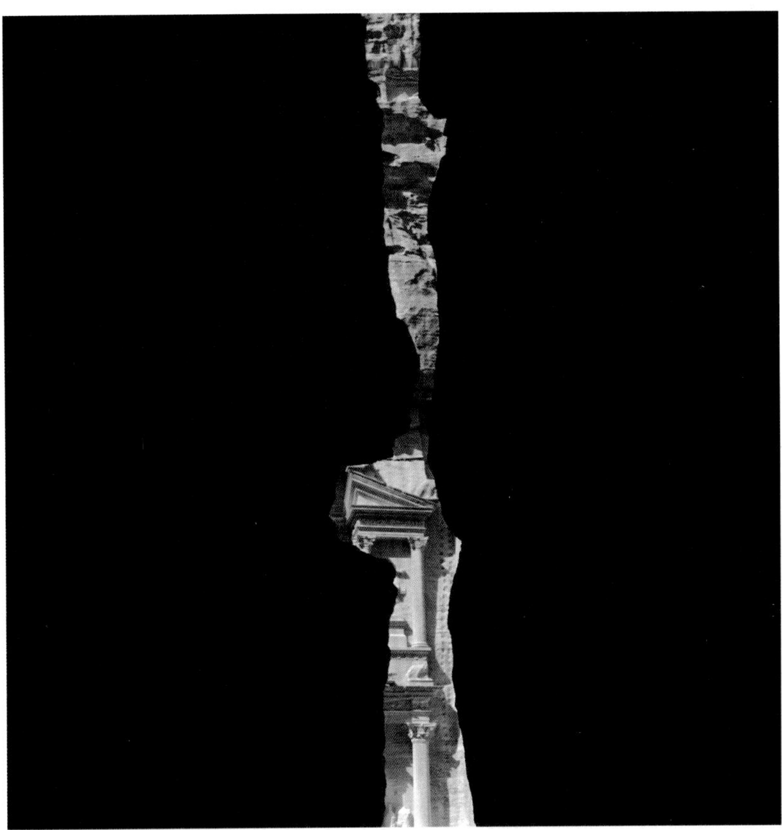

Lynn Davis, *Petra, Jordan*, 1995

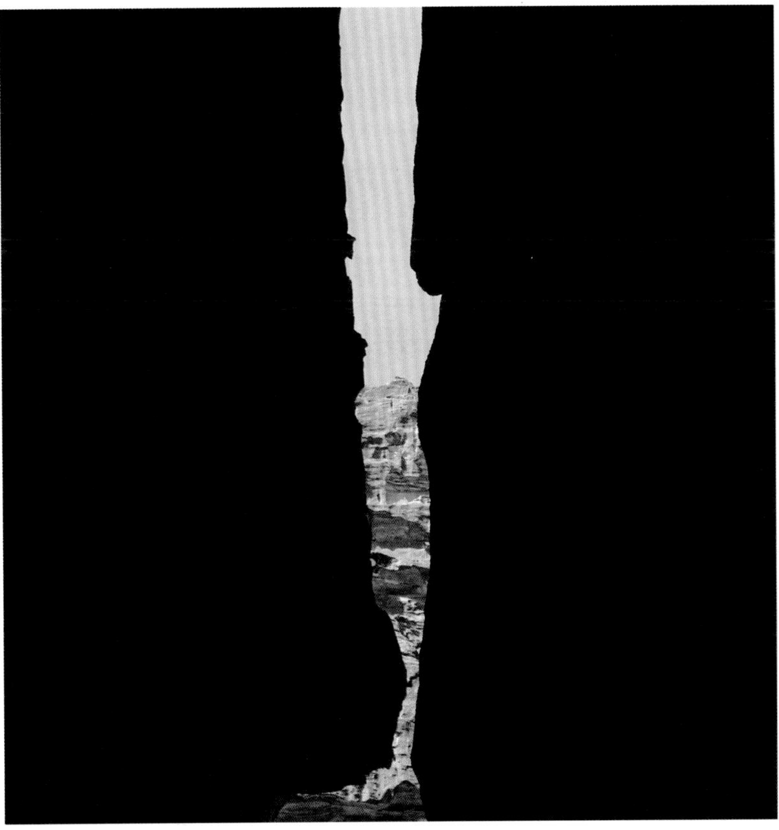

Lynn Davis, *Petra, Jordan*, 1995

Lynn Davis, *Iceberg #7*, Disko Bay, Greenland, 1988

LD: Well, after my son died, I can't imagine anything being frightening, really. It's a different perception. In fact, it's so different that sometimes, if somebody says, "Is that pleasurable or is that not?" it doesn't matter that much. The normal categories are all shifted. So, it was much more interesting than it was frightening, because I felt invisible, and I felt also like not only was I invisible but I could see through everything. Like structures of buildings seemed . . .
MH: Everything seemed sort of penetrable?
LD: Yes. And it was very strange but very fascinating, because the solid really became relative. In fact, when I was in Greenland, the great lesson I learned there when I was out floating in the middle of the night, and the light was changing, the water was moving, the icebergs were moving, I was moving, was "yes, everything is changing every second."
MH: Do you ever try to render a sense of the spiritual?
LD: No. I think it's a big trap. Whatever state is an altered state, that's something you can feel yourself. But I never go in search of it, nor do I try to photograph it. I know when I feel it. And I could say yes, I'm very interested in experiencing that, but that's it. I try to convey as succinctly as I can a sense of the magic of the place, its form, and the elements. And every place is different. Mostly, I try not to get in my own way.

Now I'd like to work more with light itself, not in the way of just making light pictures, but actually working with light. Because after this period, the elements basically are what I'm left with, and I might be able to do something with that and I might not.
MH: I want to ask you a little about the constructed world versus the natural world in your work, and how we seem to make distinctions between objects or places by naming them, therefore making them somehow tangible, I guess, but when we stop naming them they can feel so similar. . . .
LD: In a way, I construct the natural world. I really structure the natural and make it in a sense look like it almost could have been constructed in the studio, because it's that defined, and all my pictures are really very finely constructed, as if I was drawing them or painting them, or using a little mock-up. That's also why I love the square format. It's an artificial frame.

But yes, the naming of things all kind of disappears, you know. That's what is a little bit artificial in the way that I've shown my work, because every few years there's been an exhibition of work about a particular area, but in fact, I see the work in a much larger context, where everything is all mixed-up. It doesn't matter if it's a body or an iceberg, a modern building or a sacred site.

Although, I find that as much as I liked working in the studio, in the end I love the big open world, because I love the natural light, I love the wind going by, I like the coldness and the heat.
MH: And isn't there also more possibility for serendipity out there?
LD: Oh, absolutely. The great accident. You know, it's so funny, because in a certain way, the pictures do look kind of formal and beautiful, but when you realize that a lot of them are taken from horseback, from camel-back, from boat. . . . I travel with a little old Rollei that you can buy at any pawnshop. . . . Somebody left it at my house in the sixties. And I travel with that in my purse often, in a Baggie. I didn't even use a backup camera until about a year ago. I just traveled with that little camera and some film. In fact, the whole formality comes from the inner structure, not from tripods, not from being stationary . . . I don't wait for pictures. I move fast. If the light isn't happening, I move on, come back, go around. I move like a maniac when I shoot. And yet the pictures seem quite still and calm. I am very free. There are no rules. And I have to be totally instinctual. I can't be controlled by anything.
MH: So if it suddenly looks good way over there, that's where you want to be?
LD: Oh, absolutely. Like, with the icebergs, we'd be here, then we'd be twenty miles over there, then the light would change and then we'd be back over there. It's a very wild process. Then all of a sudden, it will just get very still, when everything is right and you say, "Okay, this is the time." And it's a glorious, exciting moment. Time sort of stops, and all of a sudden it feels like everything is going in slow motion. It could be a minute and a half, but it feels like about three hours, and then it's over—that's it. I think probably life is like that. What it must seem like at the end. Like, "You mean that all happened?"

Lynn Davis, *White Valley*, Cappadocia, Turkey, 1995

DOUG AND MIKE STARN

BY DIANA C. STOLL

I. A Solar System

Nothing sensible in all the world is fitter to be made an image of God than the Sun, which first illumines itself, then all the celestial and elemental bodies. . . .

—Dante Alighieri, *Paradiso,* Canto X

Doug and Mike Starn are not sun worshipers, they say, although their recent work might indicate otherwise. Like those suicidal summertime moths you find on their nightly pilgrimage toward the filament of the porch lamp, the brothers are headed inexorably toward the solar core. Their path has led them into myths, sciences, and other belief systems: from Sol Creatrix and Sol Invictus (the Roman gods of creation and victory) and the Japanese sun-goddess Amaterasu to NASA's Solar and Heliospheric Observatory (acronym SOHO); from the *Egyptian Book of the Dead* (in which the sun dies every evening to be reincarnated every morning) to Dante's light-filled Paradise.

Form follows notion in many of the Starns' sun works: scattered images and texts in light-boxes; beaming, golden planes that seem to maintain their own gravitational balance.

As the Starns point out, the presence of the sun forces into shaming scale our tiny planet. "SIZE OF EARTH," read little signposts within these glowing collages—and an arrow points to a small dot. "This shows the earth as nothing but a meaningless silhouette in the face of the sun," the brothers say. "But it also leads us through a lot of other concepts—besides the disconcerting view of humanity's goals and achievements. It shows the relative similarities of earth to sun, sun to galaxy . . . and still further, to an optimistic view of the individual and humanity." And indeed, the brothers have begun to move beyond awe of our own solar system and our place in it, to the next logical step: the place of our galaxy within the larger context of infinity. NASA has recently invited the Starns to join as official artists-in-residence of the NASA Art Program. According to the agency, previous artists in the program—including Robert Rauschenberg and James Wyeth—"have provided NASA with a historic record of achievements and have given the public a new and fuller understanding of U.S. aerospace advancements." While the Starns are not sure exactly what their role will be in this effort, they seem inspired by it. "We've been using imagery from NASA for five years, but this direct access to the engineers, scien-

SIZE OF EARTH
PLATO

II. The Music of the Spheres

The rich physical quality—the optical allure—of the Starns' work acts as a magnet with which they manage to convey us toward this dark cosmos of science, spirituality, and infinitude. The sun pieces are visually glorious: three-dimensional light-constructions, layer over layer of sparkling transparent film printed with symbols and texts both ancient and modern (from Plato's treatise citing the movement of the stars as evidence of their living souls, to a recent paper on "Particle Dynamics in Two Colliding Plasmas"). These texts are illuminated manuscripts, so to speak, incorporating heliothematic elements, such as the spiderlike image of the sun encircled by a jagged wheel of erupting plasma, and the recurrent face of the placid "Petrus Christus Frau" (an embodiment, say the brothers, of the sun itself). Recently, they have been moving further into three dimensions with their sun works, creating Plexiglas orbs, more like bubbles than planets, that contain small lights or, again, the image of the Christus Frau. They have also been investigating digital representations of the *sound* of the sun—gases moving around and steadily exploding—to accompany future sun works as an atmospheric undertone.

But, despite that physical allure, the Starns say that their work is not "purely ocular," as it has often been described. "We've always been frustrated that the work is thought of that way. Even back in art school, our intentions were to open photography up, and take away the idea of the sacrosanct two-dimensional image." There are a number of unavoidable concepts at play here, among them—an important one—the idea of *age*, and how artworks (like people, like the planet) are transmogrified as time moves on. "Art changes," they say, "not only physically but in its concept—how people think about it."

The Starns acknowledge the physicality of photography, and its fragility. They embrace time and change. Their attitude toward their own artworks is refreshingly unprecious, and they are impatient with the dogmatic perfectionism of many photographers: the doctrine of the dustless negative, the inviolable print. "We started in photography when we were in our teens," Doug says, "and we loved it except for that doctrine." They welcome dust into their pieces, and in fact they are now talking about inducing an "aging process" in their art by releasing live silverfish and bookworms into a work-on-paper atmosphere, so that the living creatures will make lacework of the piece. (In a related vein, they have also recently been photographing those suicidal moths and other light-attracted beings.) They are making a multilayered metaphor, encompassing themes of age, transformation, society, and—literally—life itself.

III. The Starns Aligning

For the past seven years, the Starns' studio has been set up in the Red Hook area of Brooklyn, just a block off the haphazard large forms and detritus of the waterfront. Their studio space is divided into sections: an enormous darkroom, a shop stacked with wood and Plexiglas—where many of their photo-and-light constructions are put together—and a central room that is scattered with more haphazard forms and detritus, as well as works in progress and finished pieces. This central space, when I saw it, was darkened, lit only by gold-glowing artworks hung at apparently random heights or propped against the wall, beaming like a surrounding constellation.

Much has been made of the Starns' identical twinship and the consequent uncanniness of their collaboration. Theirs might be the visual-arts equivalent of what musicians know as "family blend"—two voices that combine with a kind of perfection that can only be the result of genetic closeness. It's true that the Starns complete each other's sentences, and they claim that they rarely disagree when thinking through their art. "If we do," says Doug, "it usually means the piece isn't working anyway." Generally, the brothers evince a quiet, almost bashful modesty about the work, yet without a trace of diffidence.

The Starn Twins (as they were known at the start of their career, before the moniker began to grate) hit the ground running in the mid 1980s, just out of the School of the Museum of Fine Arts in Boston, with a style of work that some critics dismissed as "sentimental," and others found a relief—"sheer beauty"—in an airless postmodern climate. The sense of palpability in their work of the eighties—large photo-collages, frequently in ancient-looking sepia tones, spliced together with the Starns' signature cellophane tape—is part of what gave their art object-status. Nonetheless, many of their subjects were loaded—the Mona Lisa, a dead Christ figure by Philippe de Champaigne, a portrait by Rembrandt; for these pieces, the rubric "object" seems almost coy. Today, icons such as these are barely identifiable as images, shuttered as they are behind layers of history, culture, and interpretation; there is no escaping their conceptual substance.

Now older, sturdier perhaps on the footing of their ideas, the Starns are open about the conceptual relevance of their images. About the sun works, which unquestionably combine the scientific and the artistic with the spiritual, they say, "This is, for us, a way of bringing something personal to a universal level."

IV. Illuminated Manuscripts

"It's not enough to look at books: you actually have to read them." This dig appeared in a review in the *New York Times* in response to the Starns' 1995 exhibition of "Heliolibri" at New York's Pace/Wildenstein/MacGill Gallery. In recent years, the brothers have been incorporating texts into their collages, and more than texts, entire book-forms, page after page printed on transparent film—so that, in effect, the whole book is presented to us in a piece, all the information in a mass that cannot be sorted out in any linear way. "The idea," they explain, "is to make all the pages incorporeal, with all of the knowledge and thoughts shown at once—layered, as they're stored in your mind."

The book is an object—and these objects have plenty of visual grandeur: Renaissance tomes on the planetary systems, complete with colorful maps of the universe, delicate script of the Japanese

(continued on page 22)

Doug and Mike Starn, *Solar Plasma*, 1992–1995

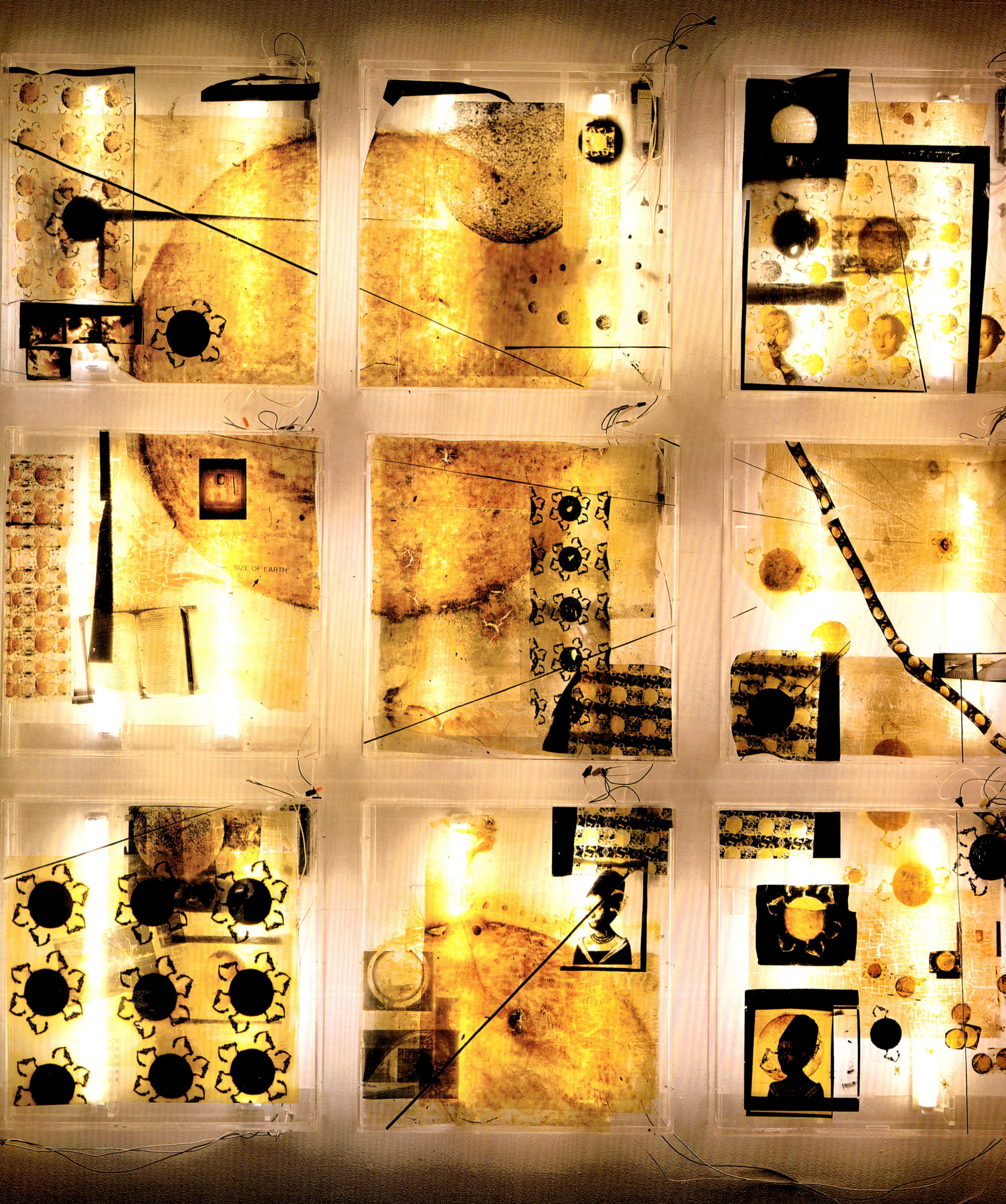
SIZE OF EARTH

Doug and Mike Starn,
Hydrogen-filled Lungs, 1996
Opposite: Doug and Mike Starn,
G.U.T. Epoch,

Usually, archaeology is artifacts or ruined structures; this is archaeology over archaeology over archaeology, of written accounts of the fighting and occupations of Jerusalem.

Above and opposite: Doug and Mike Starn, *Rampart's Café* (detail), 1995–1996

The texts are transparent so you can see the history all at once, the paper of the photographs is taken away leaving the thoughts, the events, the memories. The books are photographed page upon page, these ideas from four thousand years ago, warped, corroded, dust-filled over time.

continued from page 16)

Nihongi, the chronicle of ancient matters, withering pages from Dante's *Paradiso*, et cetera. Some of these texts come from an ancient, geocentric universe, a place of deep spirituality, where communications were set down in ciphers, in hieroglyphics, on parchment scrolls, in codices; where monks worked in *scriptoria* and scholars copied page after page of formulae and speculated about the shape of the cosmos. We do not need to read these texts for them to have an impact on us: we know that they are visitors from those bygone worlds, but that many of the passions and beliefs they reference are still very much alive in our world. The Starns say that their series of "Heliolibri" is about "accumulated knowledge, complex thought, and experience through time. They're portraits of all that." And, as with any portrait, the mute face can speak, and can tell you a certain amount (sometimes a great deal) about what is behind it.

For the third-millenium anniversary of Jerusalem last October, the Starns were asked by the Jerusalem School of Photography to create an installation at the Tower of David Museum. The result of this commission was *Rampart's Café*, a very personal reaction to the city itself. "It's a place that seems very secular, in a way, very chaotic," says Mike. "But after a while there, you get a sense of ancientness that almost seems to come up from below the streets." Following this idea, they have made a series of three Plexiglas tables, set with plates, glasses, and eating utensils. The tables might seem prosaic, if they were not transparent so that you can see what is embedded in them, right under your nose if you are seated at them: three massive texts—the Koran, the Dead Sea Scrolls, and a twelfth-century Crusader Bible—all open and tattered, lit from below with golden light. As the Starns describe it: "The texts are transparent so you can see the history all at once, and the paper of the photographs is taken away leaving the thoughts, the events, the memories." To accompany this bread breaking, the Starns have added the ambient element of sound: tapes of prayer songs and chants, which permeate the installation space—the voices of the children of light.

Illuminated manuscripts: the latest incarnation for the Starns are books of their own scrawled notes about their sun pieces—printed onto transparent film pages (which can be turned and read), woven with super-thin fiberoptic lights, glowing veins in the leaves. The light and the book have become a single entity.

The artists are not yet ready to let people read these diaries. But even without the beaming notes, it's clear that the Starns are moving further and ever further into the ineffable gravity of light. It seems, in fact, that they are closing in on the very wick.

Doug and Mike Starn, *Rampart's Café* (detail), 1995–1996

RAGHU RAI

BY MUKUL KESAVAN

I was five years old when the country was partitioned, says Raghu Rai. That makes him about fifty-five, because it's nearly half a century since that happened, that and Independence. Fifty years of freedom, with the evil frisson of genocide thrown in—it's a natural for the color pages, and every editor in India wants a piece of this anniversary.

Raghu Rai can remember running across roofs in 1947, flying from a mob with murder on its mind, because the small town in west Punjab that his family lived in had abruptly become part of another country. He thinks they fled to Amritsar, though he isn't sure, but he can clearly remember times when there wasn't enough

Life through a lens has been his textbook and he has been educated by his camera, click by click. Rai is instinctively populist in his view of photography. Unlike Strand or Cartier-Bresson he doesn't see the world as his subject; India is big enough for him.

to eat. It was a large family, ten siblings in all, and one of them, an elder brother, a photojournalist in his own right, taught him how to use a camera. Success came early; a year after starting as a news photographer, he became chief photographer of the best daily newspaper in the country at that time, the *Statesman*.

Today, Rai is a star, but before that, he is the made-good son of migrant parents, one of a million Punjabi refugees, legendary for their resilience in adversity, for their ability to build new careers out of the rubble of their post-Partition lives, and he shares with them their pride in being self-made men.

I don't read, he says more than once in the course of the conversation. He isn't confessing to illiteracy; it is his way of saying that he isn't bookish, that he doesn't depend on other people for his ideas. Life through a lens has been his textbook and he has been educated by his camera, click by click. Rai is instinctively populist in his view of photography. Unlike Strand or Cartier-Bresson he doesn't see the world as his subject; India is big enough for him. You need to know a place, a country, before you can photograph

Raghu Rai, *Praying at Twilight Time*, Old Delhi, ca. 1985

it as an insider, he says. Without that hard-won intimacy, photography becomes spectacle; thus Cartier-Bresson's Indian pictures are, for Rai, brilliant but indefinably foreign. He tried to illustrate this with an analogy from the cinema. David Lean's *Passage to India* doesn't work for Rai because Lean knows so little about the country that, besides getting social detail all wrong, India's landscape doesn't show through as panoramically as it should have done in a Lean epic. So far, Rai's instinct is true: Lean's film is almost comically inept. But then he cites *Dr. Zhivago* as a successful example of Lean's work, where the grandeur of Russia's landscape is authentically used as a backdrop for the story. The problem with this is that *(a)* Lean knew about as much about Pasternak's Soviet Union as he did about Forster's Raj and *(b) Dr. Zhivago* wasn't shot in Russia. The analogy tells us more about Rai than it does about Cartier-Bresson: like many autodidacts, Rai isn't good at theorizing his prejudices. Not reading has its down side.

Rai's credo is the photographic equivalent of social realism. A photographer's job, he says, is to cut a frame-sized slice out of the world around him, so faithfully and honestly that if he were to put it back again, life and the world would begin moving again without a blip or stutter.

Rai's credo is the photographic equivalent of social realism. A photographer's job, he says, is to cut a frame-sized slice out of the world around him, so faithfully and honestly that if he were to put it back again, life and the world would begin moving again without a blip or stutter. According to him, an older generation of Indian photographers became trapped in a sterile pictorialism, and he constantly counsels younger photographers to beware the pernicious influence of painterly ideas, ideas that encourage the making of structured, harmonized, centered images. The romance of painting has to be resisted because it retards the development of an independent aesthetic for photography. According to Rai, contemporary photography values the anarchic frame, with the action bleeding off into the edges, not tunneled into the center. For him, the evolution of photography is linear, with pictorialist mastodons ceding ground to realist primates.

He disowns much of his own output—his book on the Taj Mahal, for example—as pretty work that pandered to a tourist vision of India. Around the time he turned fifty, he undertook a reappraisal of his work. He stopped working as a photo editor for *India Today*, the country's leading news magazine, and concentrated on creating a personal, expressive body of work, free of the constraints of photojournalism.

In 1994, he produced a new book of photographs of Delhi, mainly in color. He thinks its pictures are more interesting and mark a new direction; after years of focusing on a single event and dramatizing it, he's now working more complexity into every inch of the frame, even its margins. Also his new pictures have less accessible subjects: he's made a self-conscious attempt to avoid Indian exotica—cows on main streets and other suchlike quaintnesses. People want you to become an entertainer, he says, and he finds some of his work too predictably Indian. The trouble is, he says in a plaintive aside, that much of India is like that.

He finished a book of pictures centered on Mother Teresa, and he is near the end of another book on Indian classical musicians, a project he has been working on for years. He's about to mount a retrospective of his work at the National Gallery of Modern Art in New Delhi for which he's spent nearly two months in the dark-

(continued on page 31)

Above: Raghu Rai, *On a Monsoon Day*, Delhi, 1976–1977
Opposite: Raghu Rai, *Varanasi, Ganges*, 1972

Raghu Rai, *Swami Narayan Temple*, Ahmedabad, 1990

(continued from page 26)

room, and there's no end in sight. He's his own curator; not because he wants to be—he would love to sit down with a discriminating critic and choose images representative of his oeuvre—but simply because there is no curatorial tradition in India. What he misses most working in India is not the big agencies or the big magazines, but informed critics, curators, and peers to bounce ideas off. He reckons he's lost years of growth as a photographer because of the absence of an institutionalized culture of photography, of committed contemporaries. He acknowledges few Indian precursors or peers; Sunil Janah, best known for his harrowing pictures of the Bengal famine, is almost the only photographer mentioned. Too many of the others are journeymen, unwilling, in his picturesque phrase, to smoulder in the fires of creativity. He tried to create a forum for Indian photographers, but the factionalism and self-promotion and argument that attended its birth made him withdraw.

Most of the pictures in his retrospective will be in black-and-white, though there will be a section of color photographs. His signature work was done in the eighties in black-and-white for *India Today*—vertigo-inducing images made with a wide-angle lens, where foreshortened figures from newspaper headlines dominated the center and/or keeled away toward the edges. Since then, he has divided his time between black-and-white and color, but his partiality to the former is obvious. Color, he says, is good if you're working without a specified subject. But it's limiting, because it constrains the circumstance in which you can shoot. It's hard to control, and if you're shooting a story you can't stop life to accommodate the demands of the perfect color exposure. Black-and-white is much better for that; it lets you concentrate on the subject. He pauses. Black-and-white gives you a filter that unifies the sky.

Above: Raghu Rai, *Installing Statue of Lord Mahavir*, Delhi, 1992
Left: Raghu Rai, *Imambara in Lucknow City*, 1991

Raghu Rai,
Burning Ghat,
Varanasi,
Ganges, 1994

Pages 34–41: Photographs and text by Lise Sarfati

LISE SARFATI

The ideas of memory and flight have, for me, become metaphors for evoking the current transformation of Russia. This transition period, whose resolution cannot be foreseen, has overturned all widely held clichés about the country. It is not only the end of a political regime and its ideology, but also a general destabilization—without exception—of all generations, their everyday lives, values, and souls. This break affects entire groups of the population: workers, peasants, and youth have become marginalized and have been rejected by society.

In reaction to these new circumstances, they have adopted two divergent attitudes: some live in the memory of a distant past; others run in unknown directions, trying to escape history. Both groups, those remembering and those fleeing, move toward opposite poles, like two trains on parallel platforms that will never meet. I have tried to render the movement, the transformation itself, and its impact on the bodies and minds of the Russian people. The story presented here of Aza and Alexandra, two transsexuals, reflects my concept of the flight.

I met my friend Sergei Charidjanian in Moscow. He was a photographer working for the daily Moskovskii Komsomolietz. *We were in the newspaper office and he showed me a frightening report compiled by some of his colleagues: black-and-white photographs detailing a sex-change operation. I wondered how it was possible to take such pictures, especially so close up, but mostly, I was fascinated by this idea of transformation, as it seemed an allegory of the transition period in Russia. I thought of Mikhail Bulgakov's* Heart of a Dog, *in which a stray dog is adopted by a doctor who conducts an experiment and changes the animal into a man through a human organ transplant. As a man, the good dog becomes mean, declares himself a proletarian and makes trouble for his master, who despises him in the same way the Russian elite has always despised the people. The idea of a total transformation of the human being is quasi-traditional in Russian history and culture.*

(continued on page 38)

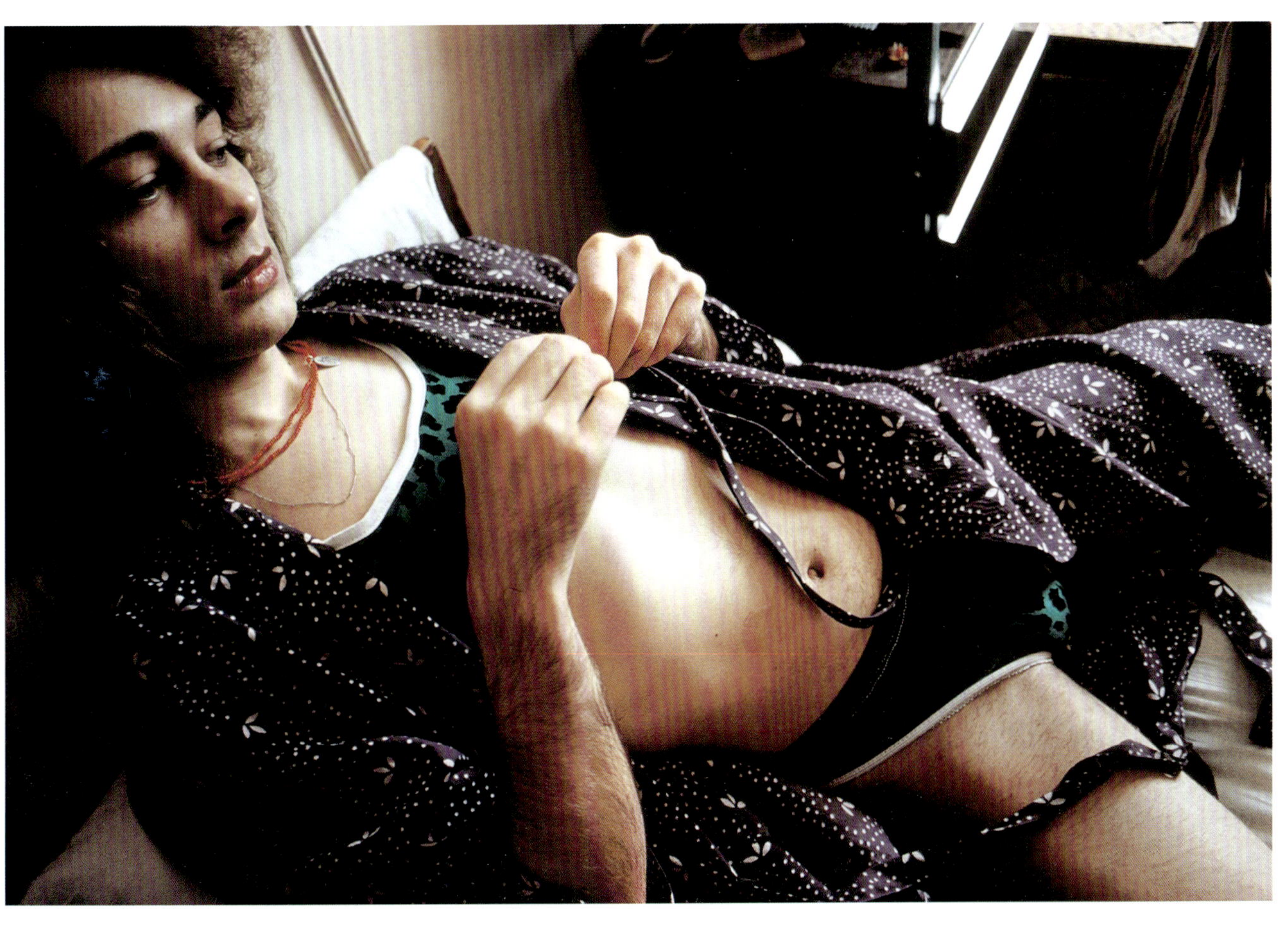

(continued from page 35)

I went to the Basseinova Hospital in Moscow. After the traditional interview with the physician in charge of sex-change operations, I was allowed to go into hospital rooms to talk with the patients. As I opened the doors of those rooms, I found myself in a nightmarish labyrinth. Their occupants were tired and often disheveled; most came from the country.

I was filled with admiration for Aza and Alexandra. The two friends were from the same remote village in Kazakhstan and had decided to come to Moscow together for their operations. I knew that in Russia's past, gays were sent to camps and lesbians to psychiatric hospitals. Now, in today's Russia, Aza and Alexandra would even get new

identity papers. But they had a long way to go: they first had to undergo a psychiatric analysis at Rostov-on-Don in order to determine whether they were really transsexuals or else schizophrenics. Then they had to find the money to pay for the operations.

Azamat was seventeen and became Aza. Alexander was twenty-four and became Alexandra. I cannot explain the magic of our relationship or the reason why they accepted me; naturally, the fact that I was a woman mattered a great deal. Whatever the reason, we had a good rapport. I don't think it had anything to do with photography. They understood that I was not a voyeur. I love to play, and they did too; they were very distrustful, like me, and also very intuitive. They recognized genuine people who did not play games with them, who respected them, and who did not fall prey to anecdotal curiosity. They understood me as a person outside of the norm, impossible to categorize.

Often, I slept in their bed while they went cruising in the hospital corridor. They were very excited by the sex change. They watched themselves in the mirror and smiled. Everything was a discovery. I felt like I had just given birth to two adult babies. They did the conventional or cliché girl things all day long: painting their nails, combing their hair, putting cushions on their stomachs to pretend that they were pregnant. They wanted to compare their genitals to mine, and I must say that in that instance, I was more shy than they were.

As the days passed, they felt stronger and decided to go back to Gelezinka, the small village in Kazakhstan where their parents lived. Aza did not work but read Tarot cards. At least she said she did, but I never saw her perform. Alexandra was a hair-dresser. We reached their village after a long trip. In the airport, Aza saw a black man for the first time. With a disgusted air, she asked me if I could go with her to take a closer look at him. She wanted to check to see if he had eyelashes.

At the village, their families were awaiting us. They didn't believe in the operation. They saw Aza and Alexandra as they had left them—dressed up in women's clothes. I stayed for a few days, then I left.

I saw Aza and Alexandra in Moscow one year later. They needed surgery again. The original sex-change operation consists of modifying genital organs and creating a vagina. Sometimes there need to be some follow-up procedures.

At the hospital, Alexandra met Andrei, a former woman who had become a man, and they got married. They went to live with his parents in the village where Andrei was born, in the Caucasus. I went to visit them some time later. It was winter and we stayed indoors. They were happy, but in the village, they were called "the transformers."

I saw Aza in Moscow one year after her second operation. She had dyed her hair platinum blond, felt sick all the time, and she barked when I wanted to take a photograph of her. I showed my pictures to the great Russian psychiatrist Boukhanovski at Rostov-on-Don, refraining from comment. After he saw Aza in the hospital, he said to me: "She is schizophrenic. She should never have had the operation."

From my encounter with Aza and Alexandra, I have put together this story as a photographic series with a single focal point: transformation. I feel that it is this point alone that allows me to share this experience.

Translated from the French by Chantall Combs

MARY ELLEN MARK

INTERVIEW BY MELISSA HARRIS

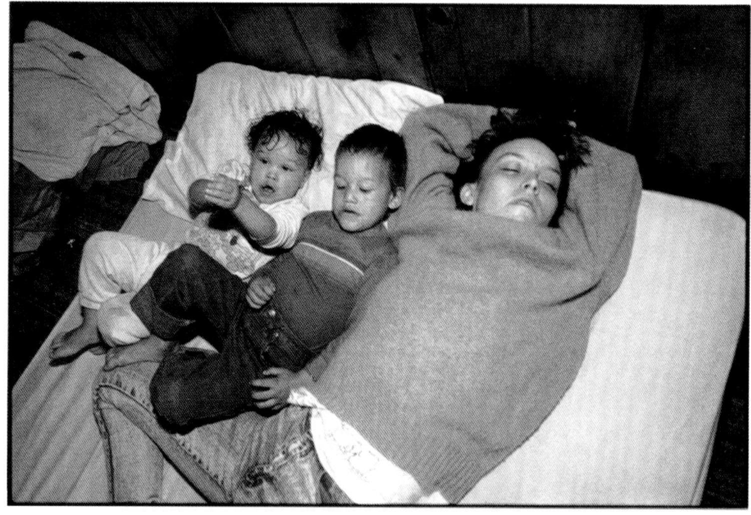

TINY: I've known Mary Ellen for about fourteen years now. I like taking pictures with her. And she's nice, she's a different type of person—outgoing and free of the world.
MH: Do you like looking at the pictures of you and your friends that were first published in her book, *Streetwise*?
TINY: I don't know. I like them, but, that was my life, and I'm more interested . . . I'm reading a book now called *Green River* that has pictures of girls, and I want to think about them, and how their lives are. I already know me.
MH: How are things for you? OK?
TINY: Oh, yeah.

MELISSA HARRIS: Children and teenagers comprise a large part of your work. What is it about them that you find so compelling?
MARY ELLEN MARK: In my pictures I like to get a sense of oddness or edginess. I think that children and teenagers are much more about that. They're growing, they're changing—especially teenagers. It's such a powerful time. There's so much rawness at that time of life, and it's really interesting to me to be able to catch that. Children and teenagers aren't so formed. Their bodies are developing, their voices are changing. They are going through so much physically during this period of time that they exhibit a real vulnerability yet, at the same time, defiance. Teenagers are very unpredictable. That fascinates me.
MH: How do you get them to trust you? Is that even an issue?
MEM: I feel with children and also with teenagers that you must never talk down to them. Even with little ones. It also helps to spend time with your subjects. I knew many of the children in this portfolio very well, but even if you're just in a location for a few moments and don't get the chance to know the people, you somehow have to take command and control—especially in a portrait situation.
MH: How do you do that without people feeling . . .
MEM: That you're bossy? You have to be a bit bossy. I don't think there's ever any formula for taking control, except that you must always be yourself. I'm not a particularly dominating person, but when I have a camera, I do take over. In order to get the image you must be assertive.
MH: Does a street child respond to you or the camera differently than a child from privileged circumstances?
MEM: Everyone is going to have a different reaction to a camera. But in some situations it is possible to get a similar reaction from a street child and a child from a very wealthy family. It all depends on the individual. Some people are very shy and not able to reveal themselves in front of the camera, and other people are just naturals. I find the shy people are often harder to photograph, because they won't allow you to see who they really are. They can be very stiff and uncomfortable. I'm shy, and therefore I can relate to that feeling—it's hard to be photographed. You have to be willing to give something of yourself.
MH: Are people who seem open in their personalities, generally open to a camera, or does one thing have nothing to do with the other?
MEM: One thing has nothing to do with the other; it really depends on the individual's ability to love the camera. Often when I'm working in documentary situations and photographing people, I find individuals who are amazing to photograph because they are able to just lay themselves wide open to you in front of a camera. You try and approach each situation with your own particular point of view and your own way of taking control. Sometimes you have to struggle to get that control. And you risk making a fool of yourself. But you won't get strong photographs unless you trust your instincts. When you go out to photograph, whether it's at the home of a very famous person or at the home of a totally unknown family living in poverty, they all want to feel that you know what you're doing. They don't want to doubt you, because they are trusting your photographic interpretation of them.
MH: Has photographing teenagers changed any of your views on certain issues, like sex education in schools, or the juvenile justice

(continued on page 48)

Mary Ellen Mark, *Chrissy Damm and Adam Johnson*, Liano, California, 1994
When I was photographing the Damm family, I would just spend all day. This is Chrissy with her boyfriend, Adam. This is in the house where they were squatting; they were no longer living in a car, but rather a shack without water or electricity. I just hung out with the kids. They were in love.
MH: What did they think of you? They've known you since they were babies, right?
MEM: I think Jesse likes us. With Chrissy, it's a little hard to tell. She is more complex. Everything is more hidden with her. She's suffered a lot more. I mean, Jesse has suffered a lot too, but somehow he's stronger; he's able to sort of deal with it. They've just been so badly treated.
Opposite: Mary Ellen Mark, *Tiny, Dayton, and La Shawndrea*, Seattle, Washington, 1989
During this time in Tiny's life, she was in a bad drug period. I spent some time with her. Some days I would have to find her, and when I tracked her down on the street this time, she was totally high. We went back to her house and she fell asleep, which is when I took the picture. A few hours later, the Child Protection Agency came and took the kids away from her—temporarily.

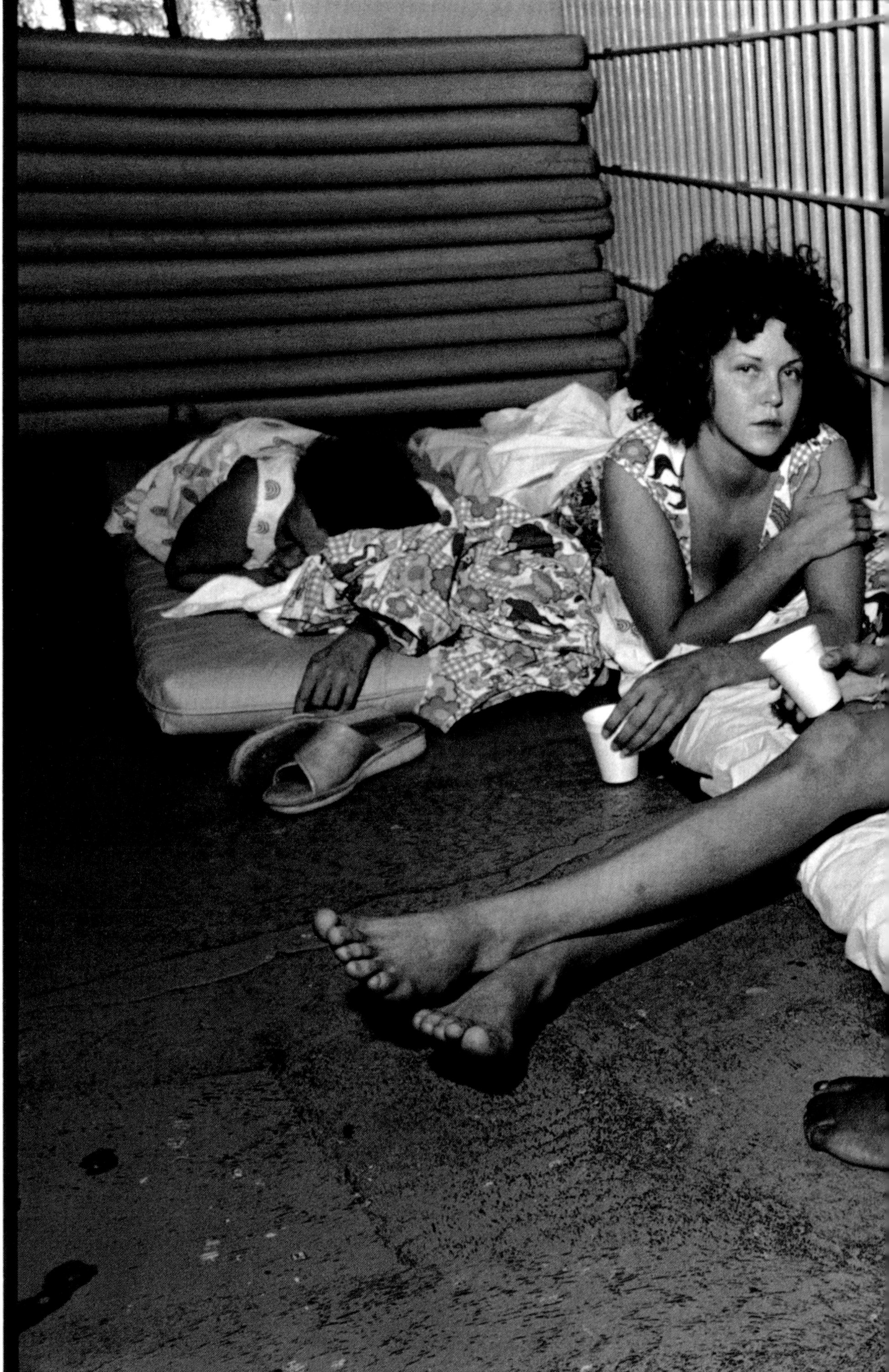

Mary Ellen Mark,
The "tank" at the Houston County Jail, Texas, 1977
I was doing a story, one of those wonderful kinds of assignments that magazines would give me years ago. The assignment was to photograph youth crime in Texas. The idea was to ride around with the police, and when a kid was arrested, to kind of stay with him or her, and find out about who the child was. It was a wonderful premise for a story, because you really see the children as people, not just as juvenile delinquents. There was a young black girl who had been arrested at a Foley's department store for shoplifting. She was actually thrown in jail. She had a child herself. It was incredible!

Mary Ellen Mark, *Wildwood*, New Jersey, 1991
Sometimes writers fictionalize reality. This was a story that the writer had suggested, saying that there was a whole community of lost kids in Wildwood, New Jersey. When I got there, they weren't there! So we just had to change the premise of the story. Instead, I did an atmospheric essay on Wildwood. There were skinheads around, and they were just so mean.

Mary Ellen Mark, *Mary Ann and Ophelia*, Mississippi, 1990
This photograph was done for Fortune *magazine for an assigned story on rural poverty, another one of those great old assignments. This picture reminds me how things have really changed. No one would ever assign a story like this now because it doesn't have "commercial viability." Everyone's thinking about "which advertisement is this tough picture going to be next to? So-and-so is not going to want a picture of a poor, sad person next to their ad." I was walking along in a cotton field in Mississippi. I just found them.*

(continued from page 42)
system, or Planned Parenthood, or welfare, for example? Do you find that outside of your aesthetic, any of your political views are informed by what you see?

MEM: Being a social-documentary photographer for so many years has educated me. It has made me realize how unfair the world is. I wish that all people had equal opportunities. I realize how difficult it is to break the cycle of poverty. Of course I would love to see somebody like Tiny have a better chance in life, and I would love to see her kids also have a chance. I wish that tragic pattern of poverty, crime, and drugs could be broken. I never feel that my pictures are about changing the world. They're just about people. I would hope that they are about people recognizing themselves in others. My photographs are more about emotions than politics.

MH: With somebody like Tiny—the protagonist of your 1988 project *Streetwise*—who you have been photographing continuously since 1983, do you feel the pictures provide some kind of reflective device for her? Do you think she looks at them?

MEM: She does look at them, because every time she loses them (which is often), she'll call me and ask for more pictures. The images of her past definitely mean a lot to her. I haven't actually seen her in a few years, and I miss her, because Tiny has a very distinctive personality. She is a real survivor, and life is still very tough for her. Her children are beautiful, and she loves them very much. I think they inspire her to be stronger.

MH: What makes you go back—to Tiny, and also to the Damm family, a story you began ten years ago with that disquieting image of them living in the car?

MEM: Well, it's really interesting going back. You can have greater access because people know you and feel comfortable with you. It's fascinating to have an overview of someone's life and to begin to understand more profoundly the changes they go through. I'd love to be able to photograph Tiny's children now and see how they've changed. She has four. One little girl named Kiyana wants to be a werewolf when she grows up. She has been saying that since she was two. I would also love to continue to photograph the Damm family. In a way, their situation was even more brutal than Tiny's. Eventually, I think, the children were taken away from the parents. I don't know what's happened to them. But I really would love to go back and photograph them again. Especially the children. I'm most interested in stories where, even though the situation is tough, I feel that there's some hope. When I photograph people like the neo-Nazis, it's difficult to go beyond the hatefulness of their outlook.

MH: With the neo-Nazis, it's obvious, but with your other subjects, do you always know their character?

MEM: You watch, you listen, and you form your own opinions. The Damm family was fascinating to photograph but most interesting because of the two older children, Chrissy and Jesse. They were just so moving and touching. They were surviving in spite of their difficult situation. It became a series of images about survival rather than a story about defeat. I'd like to think of myself as being a humanistic photographer. I prefer to photograph human beings who I feel have something that's heroic about them.

After all these years, I'm still interested in photography because I am constantly finding new ways to construct an image—to better understand that visual language. The single image with a metaphoric value appeals to me more than the traditional photo-essay. I am always trying to discover which photographs work, why they work, what is necessary to include in a photograph, and what you can leave out. Often the strongest images are those that exclude elements and leave more to the imagination.

MH: Has your language changed a lot over the years?

MEM: I hope so. The more clearly you learn how to express what you want to say and how you want to say it, the better photographer you become. I just hope that I'm going to continue to grow as a photographer. I don't want my work to become formulaic in any way.

MH: How do you find the stories? Do they all come out of assignments?

MEM: Well, life is full of stories. The problem now is finding the means to be able to produce them. Documentary projects take time, and time is expensive. In the past, magazines were my way of financing personal work. It was wonderful. I was able to produce many interesting stories and make photographs that worked for the magazine, as well as adding to my own body of work. In fact, magazine assignments were almost like grants that sponsored my work, but those kinds of social documentary assignments are harder to come by now. Publications are much less interested in documentary reality. But I am a fighter, and I refuse to look at it negatively. I love making social-documentary pictures more than ever, and I definitely intend to find other ways of sponsoring my personal work.

Mary Ellen Mark, *Coney Island*, New York, 1994
I like Coney Island. Everyone likes Coney Island. It's sort of symbolic of New York-American. I found these two Hasidic kids on the beach. I was trying a new camera and went out there to take lots of pictures.

Mary Ellen Mark,
Chrissy and Jesse Damm and Adam Johnson,
Liano, California,
1994

DUANE MICHALS

BY MICHAEL SAND

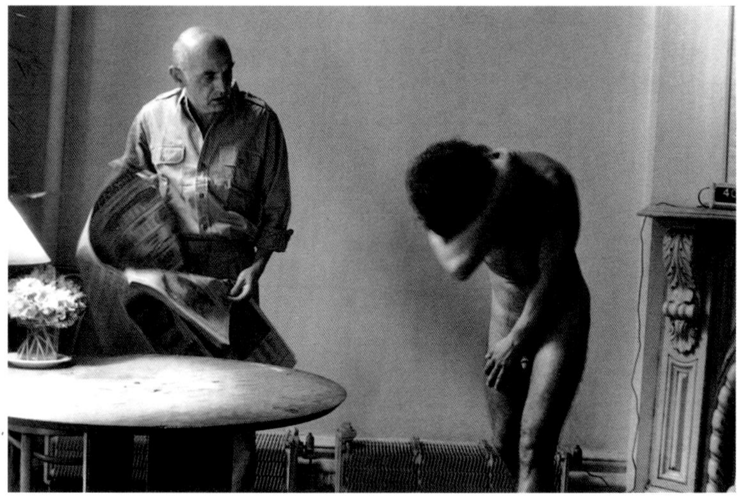

The telephone seems to bring out the antic side of Duane Michals. Once, during a drawn-out game of phone tag, he called me from the New York Public Library. "It's Uncle Duane . . . the sands of time are disappearing . . . call me. . . ." I called him back the next day and the message said he had left the city for a week. I called back a week later and the familiar voice on his answering machine piped cheerfully, "This is the good Duane Michals." Then a more somber voice cut in, "And this is the *bad* Duane Michals." The two voices began to argue with each other, finally concluding with the bad Duane cutting off the good Duane abruptly with *Leave a message!*

A few days later I found my way to the below-ground living room that he has filled floor to ceiling with books, lots of art books, children's books, and magazines. It's a wide, low-ceilinged room, with comfortable chairs and a quietude that catches you off guard in New York City. When we got around to discussing *Questions without Answers*, a book project that he was (and still is) developing, he insisted that we go into the laundry room, where, he said, the light was better. There, in the pristine whiteness, six feet below the city sidewalk but miles away in ambience, he opened the maquette for his book on top of the dryer and began to read aloud. He read as you would read to a child, with warm, avuncular charm and infinite patience. The sound of his voice filled the small room, bounced off the walls, and reverberated in my ear. His bald head and round glasses echoed the roundness of his storytelling. I began to feel a little dizzy.

Nearly a year has passed, and now I'm back at Michals's house to discuss "On Location." This time the room seems smaller. I notice that a back wall consists entirely of mirrors, and the room is actually half the size it looks. And there's Duane talking about how he doesn't believe appearances. "I don't believe portraits," he says. "If people are what they appear to be, then we would have no charlatans, we would have no politicians, we would have no priests."

Clearly he's prepped for the interview, and, at first, I hardly get a word in edgewise. He's *on*. And, of course, very engaging. He leans back, puts his feet up on the table and his hands behind his head, the stock pose of a man who wants, above all, to appear at ease. Michals's quick wit and charm come to him so naturally that it would be easy to assume that's all there is to him. But then his work over the years leaves no doubt that the jokey, charming exterior belies a man of varied composition, an artist capable of producing photographic narratives of profound philosophical wonder and poignancy, such as his classic *The Return of the Prodigal Son*, in which he plays the role of the father, undressing himself in order to protect his son from humiliation.

Understanding the limits of appearances has led Michals to a range of experiments with layered forms of expression. For over three decades now he has been challenging and delighting audiences with his particular brand of photographic art-making—staging moments rather than waiting for them; creating unusual, often very funny, and sometimes deeply personal sequences of images; and writing on the borders of his prints in that distinctive childlike scrawl. All of these devices, he feels, allow him to tell more than would the single photograph. And to get closer to the truth. "I knew my mother and father my entire lifetime," he says. "Not once did they ever reveal themselves to me. So I think a picture of my mother looking old and tired, leaning against a white wall, doesn't tell me anything about my mother. There is a difference between description and insight."

Despite his casual dismissal of traditional photographic portraiture, Michals has made his share of memorable, stand-alone images, from portraits of René Magritte and Andy Warhol to a recent portrait of artist Yayao Kusama, commissioned by the *New Yorker*. He also has had a successful career as a commercial and advertising photographer, including corporate reports and even

3

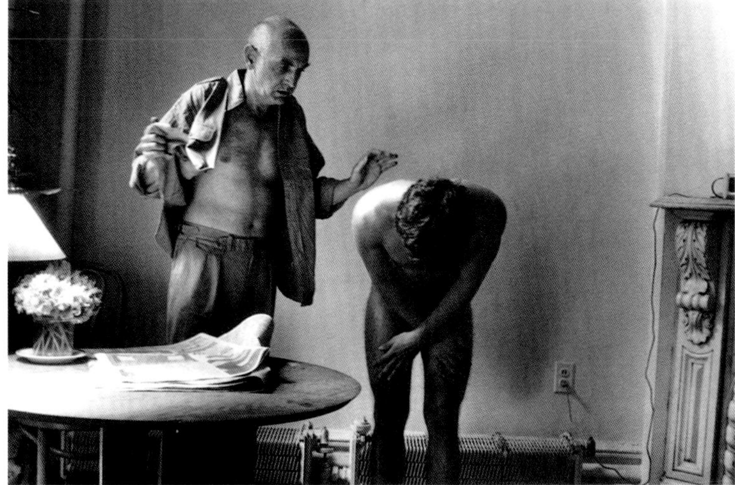

4

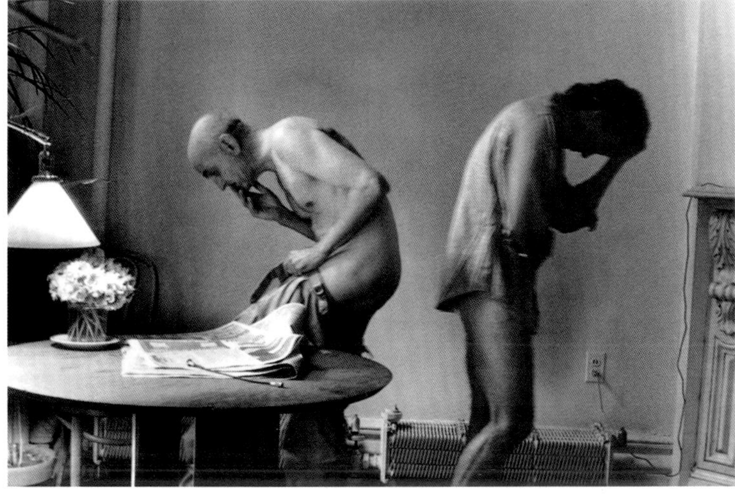

an ad campaign for Pampers. He has made an admirable life for himself for a photographer who suffers from "a frustration with the silence of the photograph."

An avid reader and a natural storyteller, Michals says that "writing, for me, is the possibility of being more intimate. I think I can be much more private in language than I can in a photograph. There's a certain presumption made about photographs, which may in fact have absolutely nothing to do with reality at all. So it's a great responsibility to write." Michals is quick to add that he doesn't consider himself a serious writer. He doesn't have literary pretensions, he says. And yet his writing is so essential to his art that if he didn't take it seriously, he wouldn't keep at it. Once again, he begins to read aloud, this time from his children's book, *Upside Down, Inside Out and Backwards*:

> *There is something I must tell you, but you don't have to listen. Of turtles' wings and sticky things and a tooth of mine that's missing. Come close so I can whisper, things I don't understand. And as I tell my tales, for naughty boys and girls, please may I hold your hand?*

Michals self-published *Upside Down* in 1993, under the Sonny Boy imprint, and he laments that it received little critical attention. The book is small and deliberately overstuffed with lots of drawings, photographs, writings, and "additional flourishes" by designer Arne Lewis. Dedicated to Edward Lear ("A giggle, a giggle for dear Edward Lear, who wrote rhymes without reason, I hear. All rules he dispensed, he despised common sense, and deemed logic to be insincere."), the book exemplifies what's complicated about Michals: a children's book that's really for adults who think like children, or perhaps for precocious children who think like adults.

"With the children's book, publishers asked right away, 'Now, is this for one-to-two-year-olds, four-to-five-year-olds?' 'No, it's for a variety of audiences,' I would say, 'it should reach all kinds of people.' Which was exactly the problem." Clearly, however, it remains one of Michals's pet projects, as he reads another passage, touching on what has become a kind of leitmotiv throughout his work, the father-son relationship: *My father could walk in the sky. He promised to teach me how. But he left without saying goodbye. I don't cry. I'm a grown-up now.*

Michals's current book project is *Salute, Walt Whitman* (forthcoming from Twin Palms at the time of this writing), a tribute to another of his longtime muses. The book consists of Whitman's poetry and Michals's photographs of an idealized young man or, alternately, an idealized boy on the verge of manhood. Michals used just one model for the project, an anonymous blond-haired youth. The photographs do not illustrate Whitman; rather they complement the poems. This is Michals's way of collaborating with a literary hero, at the same time producing new imagery. Whitman clearly looms large in his mind, and is a vehicle for his increasing willingness to explore issues of homosexuality openly in his own work.

Assuming the measured tones he reserves for reading aloud, Michals recites the opening lines from the book: *I sing the songs*

(continued on page 58)

5

WHOEVER YOU ARE NOW I PLACE MY HAND UPON YOU.

From "Song of Myself"

O span of youth! ever-push'd elasticity!
O manhood, balanced, florid and full.

My lovers suffocate me,
crowding my lips, thick in the pores of my skin,
Jostling me through streets and public halls,
coming naked to me at night,
Crying by day Ahoy! from the rocks of the river,
swinging and chirping
over my head,
Calling my name from flower-beds, vines,
tangled underbrush,
Lighting on every moment of my life,
Bussing my body with soft balsamic busses,
Noiselessly passing handfuls out of their hearts
and giving them to be mine.

—Walt Whitman

Pages 52–53: Duane Michals, *The Return of the Prodigal Son*, 1982

Pages 54–57: Duane Michals, Untitled, from *Salute, Walt Whitman*, 1996

young soldiers dream in the garden

he dead with flowers growing from their heads.

Duane Michals

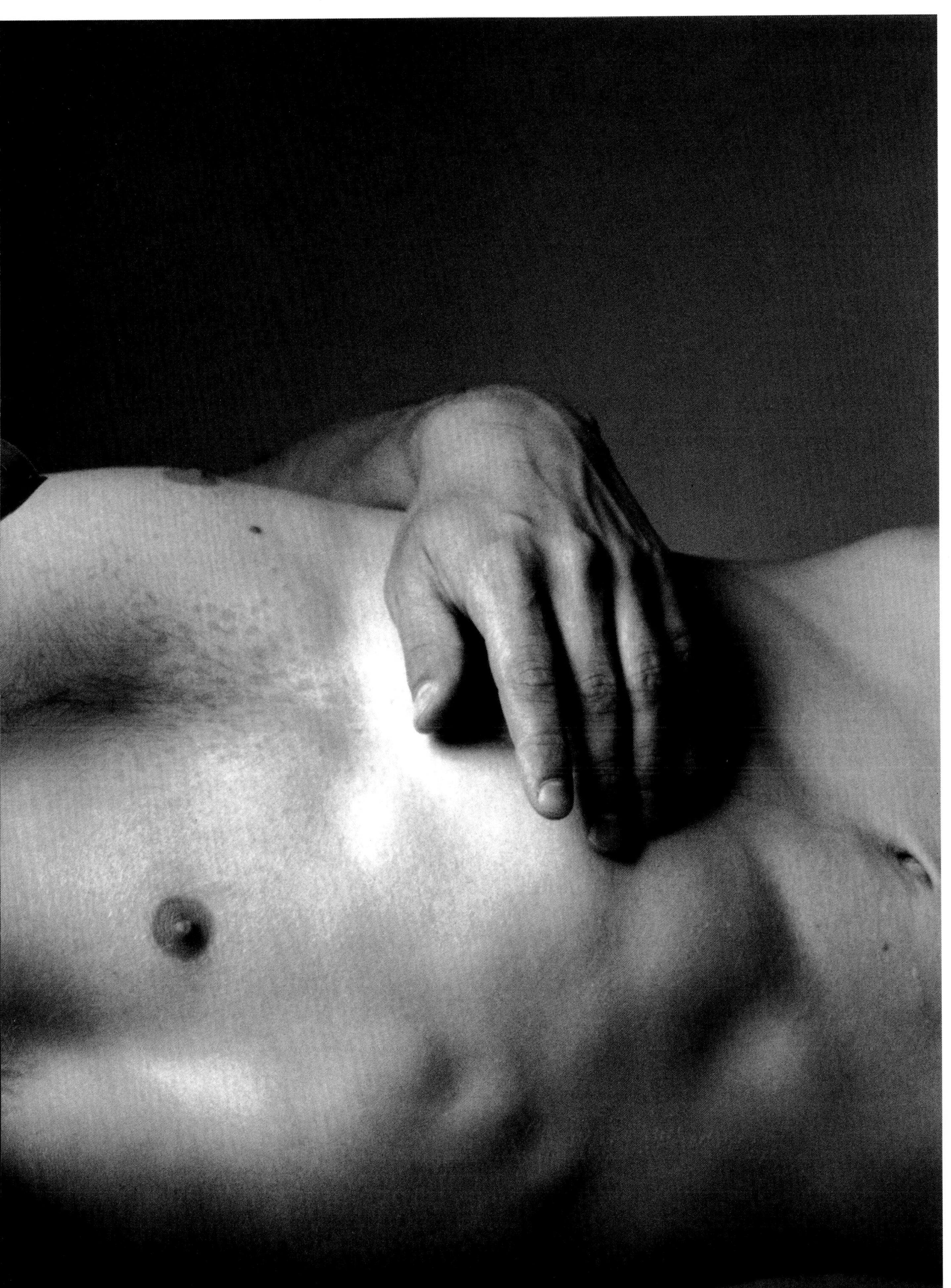

What is Desire?

Desire is a coveting need, an urgent greedy appetite to acquire an consume to satisfaction. Unlike love which lives to serve, desire is self serving and seeks its own reward. Lust is sired by a panicked yearning that erupts in passion and good sense and logic are dispensed. It is a spectre in the skin that leads the hand to sin. Desire dies when satisfied; desire denied multiplies. A rose and Circe do pose a lure to man and bee. None can resist a nectared kiss. It is their destiny. Those desired are empowered by the haunted needs of those who want. With pleasure they concede their freedom for the hope of pleasure. Young desire is raw and brash and ignites in a sudden flash. Old desire is full and ripe. It simmers slowly to delight. Green gulps, Gray sips and lingers longer on the lips. The mystery of desire resides in its primal impetus and the tension of its quest. When our days begin to hush, desire dissapates and has lost its blush, we can see that like all things, sperm too ends in worms.

I still remember even today that way your shirt was torn and I glimpsed a treasured hint of your perfect form. And with that quick glance desire was born.

(continued from page 53)

Walt Whitman sang. They ring around my mind. I recognize his cosmic slang. I am Walt Whitman's kind.

"The book is essentially about two people," says Michals. "It's about Walt Whitman and it's about this wonderful young guy I know in the country. Of course, you know, Whitman loved young men, and so it was very reasonable." Whitman's poetry appears throughout the book, frequently in Michals's handwriting on the pages of an enormous book held by the young model. "When I say, 'I am Walt Whitman's kind,'" Michals continues, "I am stating a position about my sympathy with Whitman on so many levels. But it's my take on Whitman as opposed to the Whitman anthology or Whitman for our times. This is Duane Michals's take on Whitman."

The more we talk the more I get the sense that Whitman serves as a foil for Michals's frustration regarding society's attitudes toward homosexuality. "Whitman was gay, and when he got older, he began to deny his own truth. He created this woman that he had an affair with and had children with in New Orleans. Total fiction. But then, at that time, there was no such thing as being openly gay. The word didn't even exist. Later, it was called 'the love that dare not speak its name.' It didn't have any name." Commenting on the thinly veiled homoerotic references in Whitman, it strikes me that Michals could almost be speaking of his own photography: "Of course, it's there in his poetry. And it's so sad how people try to deny it. And yet that's the very thing that gave a lot of his writing such validity, and honesty, and *bravery*."

While Michals has addressed gay subject matter in his work since early on, it has often been filtered through a screen of humor

What is Old Age?

Old age is that place in time of a life lived long, when all is past and the future's gone. Now a different song is sung, and the world is viewed from a higher rung. The soul is closer to the sun, which melts the body of its youth, sinew, bone to yellowed tooth. As the arc of age descends. Reality is less real. Vanity cannot protect nor failed ambitions be concealed. The truth has left grand dreams bereft. So much in life has lost its worth; the body stoops to greet the earth. The self's geography has changed. Lines that once were streams have been replaced by the wrinkled rivers of the face.

The body wakes one day in pain, a new sensation it cannot explain. The arteries have harden and do not pardon. The sturdy youth now needs a cane. At dawn he felt death say his name. The young man has no time to waste; the elder does not move in haste. Old age is a fragment of its prime; a summer rose in a winter's clime.

Like all events we experience, old age is by nature innocent. We define what it will be, comic turn or tragedy. Our audience is dead. With the settling of the dust, as in time all things must, the echoes of our lives are heard.

It made no sense; it seems absurd.

or metaphor. In contrast, he allows himself an almost elegiac tone in his approach to Whitman. One of the most powerful images is of the young man, lying like a fallen soldier with lilies of the valley growing out of his mouth, an image straight out of Whitman's *Speciman Days*, an account of his Civil War experiences. In fact, Michals shares many of Whitman's preoccupations—fallen or lost youth, the cruelty of war (Michals served as a second lieutenant in armor in Germany during the Korean War), and a frank embrace of human sensuality and mortality. In a stylistic shift for Michals, the book includes a number of close-up photographs of great emotional impact, violating the safe distance maintained between camera and subject in much of his earlier work.

On the back burner but always present in Michals's thoughts is the work in progress called *Questions without Answers*. Striking a note somewhere between the sensuous calm of *Salute, Walt Whitman* and the cacophonous whimsy of *Upside Down, Inside Out and Backwards*, this work is a kind of handbook of Duane Michals philosophy. The setting is an encounter in the woods between modern-day Duane and himself as a wide-eyed and wondering teenager. The young man (often represented by the same model who appears in the Whitman book) asks the senior Michals life's biggest questions: "Who Am I?" "What Is Love?" "What Are Dreams?" and Michals's oddly rhyming lines provide the answers. At sixty-four, Michals feels he has earned the right to tackle such weighty questions. Alternating between youthful inquisitiveness and mature reflection, between verbal trickery and emotional insight—between the good Duane Michals and the *bad* Duane Michals—he gets away with it.

Who Am I?

I am what is being experienced, the universe focused in the eye of the beholder. There is a quality of sensation felt as myself, which like the "I" of the hurricane is a calm center of the storm of awareness. The exact point of myself in this calm is held as if it were in a black hole, where my purest reality cannot escape itself. The Absolute. I am tethered to the Absolute by the cord of consciousness. Again and again I gaze hard at my reflection in the looking glass. Then blink without acknowledgment for my stare reveals no one is there. All descriptions of me are like barnacles attached to me. Nothing is really mine. My name is a word like any other sound, which when repeated blurs to babble. My pride enjoys the false luxury of vanity, a cosmetic decoration that casts me into the furthest ring of self-delusion. I distract myself with novelties. But they are not me. I identify with follies. But they are not me. I am an accomplice to my own ignorance. Under the magnifying glass of attention, my personality has the permanence of fog. I communicate with myself in monologue. My questions echo in my mind. All this thinking exhausts me and I must rest. But who falls asleep and dreams?

RICHARD MISRACH

BY MYRIAM WEISANG MISRACH

The color night work is new, but in a way Misrach is returning full circle to the 1970s, when he also photographed the night—minimal, moody black-and-white squares, alive with motion. Now, it's all that again: no horizon to anchor the viewer, just the gyration of heavenly bodies, their exuberant cartwheels into the dark.

It's been ten years now of this adventure, joining Richard in his travels to remarkable sites—the postapocalyptic landscape of Bravo 20; the carnage of the dead animal pits; the Edenic glory of the desert empty of humans save for the two of us. But what stands out most is the photographer's dance, that strange manic courtship between man and fading light, head swiveling under the cloth, camera roving up-and-down and side-to-side like some blind beast sniffing the air, then head reemerging, eyes wild, hair in knots and peaks, film holder in, slide out, thumb bearing down, seconds counted out—one-one thousand, two-one thousand, three . . . —then the whole thing in reverse, then running back to the van for more film, shouting with joy as he speeds by, "Can you believe this light? Oh God, I've never seen anything like that," the same exclamation each time, over the many years. The same glee.

I. The Inventory

It starts with the Volkswagen van (the fourth in twenty-five years), windows curtained off against the sun. A foam bed on the floor. Three pillows. A sleeping bag. A scratchy Mexican blanket. Several plastic gallons of Black Mountain water. Toilet paper. A roll of paper towels. A parka, permanently stored here. A dog-eared Rand McNally road atlas. Several topographic maps. A shovel. An axe. Jumper cables. An entire suitcase of books by Baudrillard, Ballard, Camus, Pound, plus a book on the stars called *Mapping the Heavens* and a planisphere. And music: lots of Philip Glass and Steve Reich, along with Santana, Nick Cave, John Adams. Anna Domino, Dylan, Blind Melon, Smashing Pumpkins. There's also a tape of Richard's son, Jake, playing Mozart on the clarinet,

Richard Misrach, *Venus and Missile Evasion Flares from Gu Oidak (Big Field), Tohono O'Odham (Papago) Indian Reservation, 3.19.96 8:29 P.M.–10:18 P.M.*, Arizona

Richard Misrach, *Moon over Dead Mountains, 11.2.95 6:17 P.M.–6:57 P.M.*, California

and gifts from friends who compile what they call "driving music," each assortment wondrous and unique.

Then, of course, there's the 8-by-10-inch Dierdorff camera, which starts the trip shrouded in the dark cloth, folded inside a battered thrift-store suitcase (cost: $3.50), Richard being of the opinion that no one would ever steal this old thing. So far he has been right. There's the heavy Gitzo tripod, three large Coleman coolers, two for the neatly stacked boxes of 8-by-10-inch film and the twenty-five film holders, the third one for food storage.

II. The Process

WAITING: "What does he do all day?" my dad used to ask. Hard to explain. He travels nonstop for many hours, until he gets to a particular spot. Actually, he doesn't always know where he is going. Most of the time he has no idea. He just bumps along the highway, until something in the distance catches his eye, or there's one dirt road that seems more attractive than another, or he has to go to the bathroom. Once he gets somewhere, he sits, or lies down in the back of the van, doors wide open. Unless the light happens to be perfect, out come the books, or he writes in his notebook, or naps. Toward late afternoon, he begins to watch the light. He walks around, his head a periscope, scanning, squinting. At some point he comes running back for the camera. Occasionally he jumps into the van, slams the door shut, and speeds off into the land. Pointing at something on the horizon, he'll say, "In a while, this whole range should turn bright red, it will be fantastic." About half the time he is wrong. Nothing comes of the sunset, the sky fills with gray the light falls flat. Or the wind suddenly gusts after the stillness of the day. He can be philosophical about it. Typically, though, he rails against the elements.

PROTECTING FILM: The most important cargo on the trip is the film. Even a camera can be replaced. But film is fragile, hard to obtain, and must constantly be kept cold and dry. Several times an hour he runs his hands over the coolers, trying to assess if they're getting too hot. For the past two torrid summers—the temperature never dipping below one hundred degrees, combined with humidity, highly unusual for the desert—he was forced to take motel rooms during the day, not so much for himself as for the precious film. Still, a lot of it was destroyed, two trips in a row. A heartbreak. He has a whole series—a new canto?—he calls "contaminated film." Disasters happen, not so much in the field as in the lab. Streaks and spots manifest and spread like a miasma across the negatives. Technicians puzzle. Specialists are called in. The work stops. Between developing, contacting, selecting, and printing, often years elapse. Out of the approximately 1,000 to 1,500 negatives he shoots per year, perhaps forty-five to fifty will be deemed acceptable.

Richard Misrach, *Hyakutake and Polaris from East Mesa, 3.26.96 4:22* A.M.–*4:44* A.M., California

Richard Misrach, *Cygnus (Northern Cross) from Ten-Mile Wash,*
3.23.96–3.24.96 11:31 P.M.–1:48 A.M., Arizona

Richard Misrach, *Ursa Major (Big Dipper) from Gu Oidak (Big Field), Tohono O'Odham (Papago) Indian Reservation, 3.22.96 6:00 A.M.–6:18 A.M.*, Arizona

CHANGING FILM: The changing bag, a contraption that looks like a pup tent, is rarely used. Nor does he change film in the van anymore—too complicated. Gone are the times when I told stories in the dark to keep him alert while the painstaking, hour-long task went on behind my back. Now, he sometimes commandeers a rest room in some forlorn market or gas station: "Do you mind if I use your bathroom for about forty-five minutes? No, I don't use chemicals, I just have to take the film out of these plastic holders, and seal it in these boxes. Thanks!" More often, however, he changes film at a motel, preferably a Motel 6, because he is guaranteed a windowless bathroom.

CALLING HOME: He calls Jake a couple of times a week, trying to maintain parental contact across time and distance. He checks on the homework, the tests, music practice, panicked that maybe he shouldn't be away so much, and so he overdoes it, coming on too strong sometimes—but Jake is used to it. He calls me at least every other day. We make complicated plans: "If I don't call you tonight, that means I'm spending the night out there and I'll call you in the morning after ten and before noon, unless I decide to stay the whole day, in which case I'll find you somehow, the main thing is, don't worry." "Out there" is scary, one of the reasons I want him to call as often as possible. He has gotten stuck a few times. Once, on the Bravo 20 bombing range, the battery died forty miles from the highway. No one would come looking for him, not even the military. *Especially* not the military. So he decided to let the van sit till the next day. In the morning, improbably, the engine turned over. Another time, in the middle of nowhere on a dry riverbed, the wheels sank into a sand bar. He piled stones under them, let almost all of the air out the tires for better traction, and inched out of the trap. At this point, we live for the day cellular-phone transmission reaches into every corner of the wilderness. Until then, I follow his route on my atlas while he gives me directions from a pay phone: "It's a small unnamed playa between the Nevada border and the Sevier dry lake, not too far off Highway 50. Can you find the Wah Wah Mountains? Confusion Range? Somewhere in there." Incredibly vague information, but hopefully of some use to a rescue party.

III. Desert Canto XXI: "Heavenly Bodies [sic]"

The color night work is new, but in a way he is returning full circle to the 1970s, when he also photographed the night—minimal, moody black-and-white squares, alive with motion. Now, it's all that again: no horizon to anchor the viewer, just the gyration of heavenly bodies, their exuberant cartwheels into the dark.

For him, this is the natural continuation of "Desert Cantos"—the desert as cultural metaphor—and of the daytime sky series

(continued on page 70)

6.28.96

UNNAMED PLAYA, UTAH

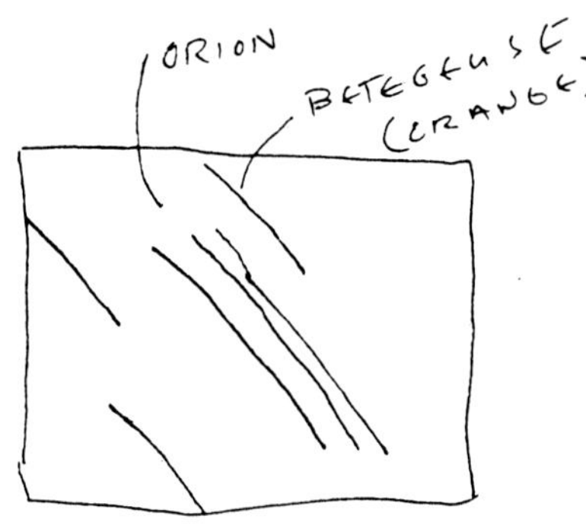

ORION FROM DEVIL'S HOLE

VENUS FROM VIRGIN VALLEY

IT'S REMARKABLE HOW MY 8 X 10 CAN ACTUALLY RECORD THE COLOR TEMPERATURES OF THE STARS -- REDS, YELLOWS, BLUES. THE FACT THAT THE COLORS, OR THE PERFECT LINES, ONLY BECOME VISIBLE AFTER I'VE PROCESSED THE FILM IS EQUALLY AMAZING. I NEVER KNOW WHAT I'M PHOTOGRAPHING - I HAVE TO ANTICIPATE THE FINAL RESULT - AND I'M ALWAYS SURPRIZED. BUT THE MOST ASTONISHING ASPECT OF ALL THIS IS HOW TRULY REMARKABLE AND AWESOME THE DESERT NIGHT SKY IS. AFTER ALL THESE YEARS I'M STILL NOT JADED. THANK GOD!)

9.1.96

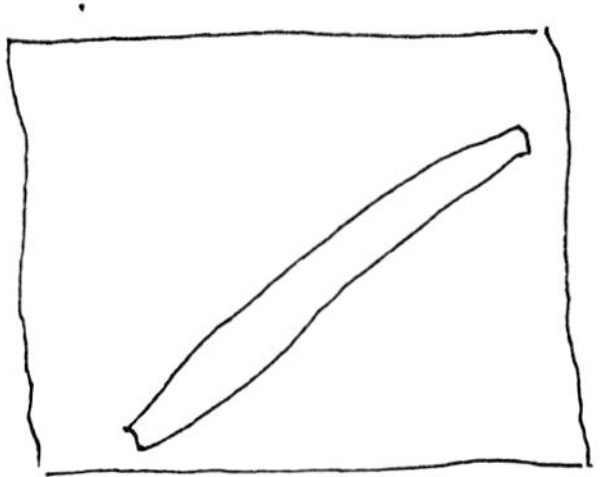

MOON FROM BLACK ROCK (2 HRS 28 MINS.)

10,000 PEOPLE CONVERGED ON THE BLACK ROCK PLAYA TO PARTY AROUND THE BURNING MAN EVENT. WITH VISIBILITY REDUCED TO ZERO BECAUSE OF THE HUGE DUST CLOUD CREATED BY 1,000's OF CARS I WAS FORCED TO NAVIGATE 10 MILES BY THE STARS. FORTUNATELY, I HAD BEEN PHOTOGRAPHING JUPITER AND ARCTURUS FOR THE PREVIOUS 3 DAYS AND THEY GUIDED ME OFF THE PLAYA. IT REALLY WORKED!

Opposite: Richard Misrach, a page from his "Sky Book"

Richard Misrach, *Venus over Virgin Valley, 9.25.95 7:29 P.M.–[8:29 P.M.]*, Oregon

(continued from page 67)
which looks at the way the land was named. He tells me about the christening of the heavens—Greek and Roman mythological notions, Latin translated into English, Ursa Major into the Big Dipper, Western ideas imposed on the celestial geography—and how that has a bearing on our understanding of the West and our culture. The native people did not use those languages, obviously. They had their own. He has just found out that the Papago Indians of Arizona took back their original name, Tohono O'Odham, and set about doing the same thing with their land, reclaiming their cultural heritage. He is fascinated with language, the way it plays against itself, its layered puzzles. "What I want to do is photograph, say, Ursa Major, next to Polaris over Gu Oidak on the Tohono O'Odham reservation, in Arizona."

Choosing the site for the skies—daytime and nighttime—is a different process from his previous practice of letting the landscape guide him. Now he chooses the place from the name on the map. Once he gets there he sets up camp and studies the sky, identifying the stars by sight or from a stellar map, anticipating the angles and arcs they will perform. The camera is eventually pointed in a particular direction and focused on a single star with a magnifying loop, an arduous job. He cannot "stop-down" and must leave the lens wide open or the film will not record a thing. The exposure lasts anywhere from twenty minutes to seven hours. Meanwhile, during the night, the wind may come up, shaking the camera, possibly knocking it over, or at the very least blurring everything; clouds may materialize and play hide-and-seek with the moon; the military, on maneuvers, may shoot off missile-evasion flares that spread like brush fires across the film. He tries to catch some sleep between exposures, setting the alarm on his wristwatch. Waking up, he is so groggy he makes mistakes like forgetting to put the slide back into the holder, storing the film exposed in his bag, and then cursing when he discovers the smooth surface under his fingertips. Another night, he closes his eyes for a few minutes and wakes up two hours later under a brilliant sun, completely destroying the subtle night exposure.

The most stunning discovery about the stars is the diversity and intensity of their colors—not obvious to the naked eye. It is only when the film is contacted that Richard truly comprehends the glorious animation of the sky he has—at least intuitively—witnessed. The stars emerge—ocher, silver, lemon, green, ice blue, cinnabar—chromatic incisions revealing their age, their chemistry, their temperature. Perfectly etched lines, the heavens trace their own history for the camera to record.

Richard Misrach, *Polaris (North Star) and Ursa Major (Big Dipper) from Pisinimo, Tohono O'Odham (Papago) Indian Reservation, 3.22.96 8:38 P.M.–9:01 P.M.*, Arizona

PEOPLE & IDEAS

HOODED CAMERA

by Victor Anant

Photographs terrify me. They are, if I may coin a phrase, light-mares. By which I mean that they illuminate what is already visible to me and, in that same instant, turn my eyes into sockets.

They terrify me the same way in which the stuffed head of a lion or a tiger on a wall terrifies me. I can wrench myself awake, screaming, sweating, from a nightmare in which, for example, I am being castrated, and I can breathe myself back into my own body. When I look at a photograph I see death as a taxidermist: I see my own body stuffed with sunlight cock and balls of woven fire.

The photograph is death at first sight.

Come, die with me, as I died with the first photograph I saw taken: grandmother, Kunjamma, little mother. Come into a small one-room-and-kitchen tenement flat in the suburbs of Bombay. The hooded cobra-camera . . . 1936 . . . ?

She had borne seventeen children and had seen eleven of them die. I once asked her about the dead ones, and she narrated, as if counting the beads on her rosary, without naming any of the eleven, "snakebite, drowned, cholera, plague, diarrhea, snakebite. . . ." Their passage through her was the pilgrimage of a clan, our Brahmin clan.

There was not a single picture, calendar, image, not even a mirror, in our ancestral home in a village in Kerala, where I grew up with aunts and uncles and a dozen or so cousins. All the sounds, events, images, fleeting scenes of marriages, religious rituals, even smells like sandalwood paste are contained in her.

She could see in the dark. And she gave me her eyes. In the early hours of the morning she would wake me up and lead me through the vegetable patches, past the banana groves and the boathouse, to the exact spot where she had heard, in her sleep, a ripe honey-mango fall. If it were left until dawn the crows would peck it clean.

She was jackfruit with its hardened-nipple seeds and its riverbed of sweet flesh. She was the huge copper cauldron at the back of the kitchen in which rice was boiled for *kanjee* for our peasant laborers and the household. She was the well from which she alone drew water. She ruled with her shaved, widow head and her elephant-ear breasts and peering eyes. She was everywhere. She was the planet of my discovery of existence.

All the horoscopes of our clan, engraved on dried coconut sheaves, were kept in the wooden casket of her belly, just as all the jars of pickled mango and chilies, and fried banana and tapioca chips, were stored in the huge teakwood chest in the dark pantry to which only she had right of access. All the wisdom of our Brahmin ancestors was sealed in the shell of her scalp.

Why did she finally consent to come and stay with us for a few days in the small railway flat to which my father was entitled in a junction town near Bombay?

I think he threatened her. I think he told her that if she didn't come to us he would never take us on our annual summer pilgrimage back to our village in the deep south of India. Such a threat was, for her, living absence, unacceptable, she who had ground death between her thighs and spoke of it as an accomplishment of life. I think it was also because she had a premonition: she was ready to leave, and she wanted to see every place on earth where she had left a little of herself. My father had left the village for work in the city of gold, and to give his children the chance of an education to live in modern times.

From the day she arrived, Kunjamma created a turmoil. First, she was horrified that there was no river running through the flat. "Water in chains," she screamed, looking at the taps in the kitchen and the bathroom, "water like mice hidden in the walls? You expect me to wash with water that is perhaps not even wet?"

Although we laughed, and father collected water in a bucket and said she could make the water run over her like a stream, she would have none of it.

The next melodrama was enacted in the lavatory in the flat, which was a hole in the floor of a small white-tiled room. "No, no, no," she shouted, "I will only squat on earth."

With great patience my father eased the situation by taking her two miles away, across the main road, through wandering alleys, to a small Hindu temple which had a water tank and some wild vegetation around its walls.

Finally, there was the electric lighting. She called it the "light with false teeth." He decided that during her stay with us we would only light the brass lamp in the kitchen and would place earthenware, oil-wick bowls around the living room.

Father kept it a secret from us that he had asked a photographer to make a portrait of Kunjamma for our flat.

The evening when the photographer came, my father met him outside our flat and asked him to wait in the open yard at the back of the tenement block. He told him to select the spot where he wanted her to sit, if possible under the jambul tree where the light was good at that time. "Set up your equipment. I will give you a chair to focus. Be ready when I bring her out. She is a very obstinate woman. Don't tell her what you will be doing. If she doesn't agree I will, of course, still pay your fee."

The cameraman was a Brahmin, with a sacred thread across his bare chest, ash lines of our caste on his forehead, arms, and torso. Oiled hair, parted in the middle, the very smell of sanctity. He mounted his camera on his tripod, placed the chair at the distance he wanted, and waited. Soon he was surrounded by a babble of servants, children, parents, and passersby in the neighborhood.

My father ushered grandmother out of the flat. He used a ploy. He told her that the neighbors were seeking *darshan*, audience of her, because they had heard

Raghu Rai, *Girdhari Lal Being Photographed in Old Delhi*, 1982

she was from a venerated Brahmin family in the south. It would take only a few minutes, he reassured her. She could sit on a chair.

Giving audience is a role to which she was not only accustomed but is also a Brahmin obligation. She came out in her transparent Mysore silk wraparound, her oiled, brown skin glowing in the evening light. For a moment, after she sat on the chair facing the eager eyes of the children and our neighbors, there was tension.

"What is he doing?" she asked, pointing at the Brahmin photographer who was already bent behind his tripod, face covered by his black hood.

My father went up to the photographer and asked him to get it over with as quickly as possible. The photographer crawled out from under the hood, straightened up, smiled, folded his hands in salutation to her, moved to the right of the camera, and took the cord between his fingers.

"Ask her to smile," he told my father.

"Please smile, Kunjamma," my father said.

Grandmother looked forbiddingly stern.

"Smile? What is there to smile at?"

My father's wit came to his rescue. "They want to see your teeth," he said. It was a joke they shared.

"My teeth, here, let them look," she said, and grinned toothlessly.

Click. She was startled by the whir of the camera. It was done. Everyone around clapped.

"Once more, please," said the photographer. But she would have none of it. She got up from the chair and walked back into our flat, blessing the children.

Two days later my father brought the portrait of grandmother home. It was wrapped in newspaper, eight inches by six, framed in black. Every wave of her body was revealed. Arms on her lap, white fingers like the butter floating to the top of the buttermilk pot she churned. Her legs firmly around an invisible clay pot. Bare feet, with toes thrust into the camera. Wraparound silk and skin on a loom of light. Toothless. Not a twitch.

My father measured a nail for the picture at about her eye level. There was not a calendar, a picture, a photograph, even a mirror, in the living room of our tenement flat. He started hammering in a nail. Then he adjusted the portrait of Kunjamma.

She was sitting in the kitchen, praying with her beads, and asked, "What is that noise? I can hear the walls cracking."

"Come and look," my father said.

She rose. Stood in front of her portrait. Squinted. Eyes creased. Stepped back. Squinted again. She sat on the floor and looked up at the photograph of herself. Then she drew the same chair as in the picture and sat on it in the same way. Stared. Grinned toothlessly.

We stood around in silence. My father was clearly nervous, playing with the hammer in his hand.

"You don't like it?" he asked.

Without a trace of accusation or reprimand in her voice Kunjamma said, "My son, I will not die like this, before my appointed time, like this, on a wall, so far away from our home, upright, in black and white, with no sandalwood fire or the smell of burning flesh. No. I will be carried as all those before us have been to the burning ghat on the riverbank to join those of whose flame I am a flicker."

My father touched her feet and turned the photograph round to the wall.

The next day we saw her off on a train from Bombay back to our village, with a servant in the third-class compartment next to hers to accompany her.

She did not die until the next summer when we went back to our village for our holidays. I was there.

That morning, as usual, we went together to bathe in the river. All day she told me stories. In the evening she lay on her straw mat and said she didn't need two bananas, I could eat the other, nor a whole tumbler of milk, I could have half. Usually, at night, I assumed she would ask me to sleep beside her. That night she said, "Go and sleep. Go." Not, as we normally say when we part, "I will go and come."

I look at photographs with grandmother's eyes: as she would look at a shadow on the grass path when we went to bathe in the river, shouting, "Who are you, *vadigan*, why do you pollute my path, you untouchable?"

Of course, since then, I have stepped into many little photographic booths. At street corners, railway stations, airports. I draw the screen. I read the instructions. I adjust the revolving stool. I put in coins. Sit upright, try to smile. Press the button and wait for the flash.

WILLIAM MORRIS: THE EARTHLY PARADOX

by Mark Haworth-Booth

Frederick Hollyer, *William Morris*, n.d.

"William Morris" exhibition, Victoria and Albert Museum, London, Summer 1996

The great Victorian designer William Morris was best known in his own time as the poet who wrote *The Earthly Paradise*. When he died in 1896, Morris was described by a satirical magazine as "the earthly paradox." One hundred years on, Morris can still seem a mass of contradictions: the atheist who made the most beautiful stained-glass windows of the age, the progressive designer who thought the Middle Ages did everything better, the genial apostle of good fellowship whose private life became an unhappy solitude, and the revolutionary socialist who manufactured luxurious furnishings for the rich. ("The swinish luxury of the rich" was the precise phrase he used to explain the situation to one of his most wealthy and enthusiastic clients.)

As Shakespeare is to English literature and Constable is to English painting, so Morris is to what he called the minor arts. Morris is more like Shakespeare than Constable in that his reputation and inspiration are felt worldwide. During the summer of the centenary of his death, more than 200,000 visitors saw the William Morris exhibition, sponsored by Pearson, at London's Victoria and Albert Museum. The two books of press cuttings are of telephone-directory bulk. The enormous exhibition, organized by Linda Parry of the museum's Textiles and Dress Department, was accompanied by a catalog, edited by Parry, which drew on the specialist knowledge of fifteen other scholars. Among them was Fiona MacCarthy, author of the acclaimed Morris biography published in 1994. She has reminded us that Morris's ideas are still alive and dangerous. Wes Jackson's books, such as *Becoming Native to This Place* (1994), are on Morris's wavelength. The exhibition and its catalog embraced all of Morris's fields of endeavor and excellence: painting, drawing, furniture, church decoration and stained glass, domestic decoration, tiles and tableware, wallpaper, textiles, calligraphy and printing. Morris was not just Morris, of course, but the businesses Morris, Marshall, Faulkner & Co. and later Morris & Co., with a shop on Oxford Street and a factory in southwest London.

The exhibition included detailed displays on woodblock printing, weaving, dyeing, and type design, all crafts mastered by Morris himself. There were also sections on Morris's political activism, on his profoundly important work in conservation, and on his poetry—"Well, if this is poetry, it is very easy to write," he engagingly remarked of his earliest attempts. In March 1877, Morris took a leading role in founding the Society for the Protection of Ancient Buildings, which he abbreviated to "Anti-Scrape," by writing a caustic letter to the *Times*: "My eye just now caught the word 'restoration' in the morning paper, and on looking closer I saw that this time it is nothing less than the Minster of Tewkesbury that is to be destroyed by Sir Gilbert Scott." Although some of my best friends would not cross the street to see a William Morris exhibition—perhaps thinking of him as a wearying medievalizer or a mere maestro of chintz—he was and is a force for good. Even the fine sans-serif lettering on the London buses (Edward Johnston, 1915) owes something to Morris. We are all the beneficiaries of his fierce integrity, his commitment to decency in everything.

If what I have just written is true, how does it apply to photography? Morris's legacy is so abundant that a superb exhibition of his work was organized from Canadian sources alone by the Art Gallery of Ontario in 1993: "The Earthly Paradise: Arts and Crafts by William Morris and his Circle from Canadian Collections." The exhibition and book con-

Photographer unknown, *Portrait of Jane Morris* (from the Rossetti album), 1865

tained a section on photography, with an essay by Maia-Mari Sutnik. Sutnik rightly concentrated on the remarkable photographs of Jane Morris taken by John R. Parsons at the direction of Dante Gabriel Rossetti in 1865, on the Rossetti family photographs taken by Lewis Carroll, on the portraits of Morris and his circle by Frederick Hollyer, and on the photographs of Kelmscott Manor taken in 1896—shortly before Morris died—by Frederick H. Evans. She also emphasized the role of the photographer and process-engraver Emery Walker (1851–1933), "whose photographically illustrated lecture on typography influenced Morris's eventual commitment to printing." Morris realized that he could study fifteenth-century letterforms from Walker's photographic enlargements—and that he could draw his own designs on the same large scale. They would then be photographically reduced. Excellent as Sutnik's essay is, she missed part of the story. She assumed that Morris, so profoundly influenced by Ruskin, would have disliked photography: "One can speculate that Morris was not inspired by photographically illustrated books and folios produced by the many evolving high-quality photomechanical processes, and possibly saw photography as simply the outcome of scientific and mechanical progress. . . . It may be telling that Morris broke his silence on the subject of photography only to express some alarm at the prospect of being photographed: "I have never mustered courage enough to get my photograph taken [he wrote, not quite accurately, in 1869]; I suppose I shall soon; Mrs. Cameron threatened me with the operation . . . I don't suppose I shall escape long."

Frederick H. Evans, *Untitled* (in the attics, Kelmscott Manor), 1896

However, the story of Morris and photography began much earlier. Ray Watkinson, writing on Morris and painting in the V&A catalog, described the important journey to France undertaken by Morris and Edward Burne-Jones in 1855. As they explored the cathedrals both young men began to understand their true vocations: "At Le Havre, Burne-Jones knew and said he could not be a priest but must be a painter. Morris too rejected ordination: for him, not painting but architecture would give creative vent to all his passionate learning." While Burne-Jones drew the great churches, Morris bought photographs. Afterward he wrote the essay "The Shadows of Amiens." The article was published in February 1856 in a new journal Morris launched with his friends, the *Oxford and Cambridge Magazine*. The title of the essay is probably derived from the photographs bought at Amiens: "And here let me say something about the way in which I have taken this description upon me; for I did not write it at Amiens; moreover if I had described it from the bare reminiscences of the church, I should have been able to say little enough about the most interesting part of all, the sculptures, namely; so, though remembering well enough the general effect of the whole, and very distinctly statues and faces, nay, leaves and flower knots, here and there; yet, the external sculptures I am describing as well as I can from such photographs as I have; and these as everybody knows, though very distinct and faithful, when they show anything at all, yet in some places where the shadows are deep, show simply nothing. They tell me too nothing whatever of the color of the buildings; in fact their brown and yellow is as unlike as possible to the grey of Amiens. So, for the facts of form, I have to look at my photographs; for the facts of colour I have to try and remember the day or two I spent at Amiens, and the reference to the former has considerably dulled my memory of the latter." (p. 103) Later he reflects on the sense of awe he felt on seeing the great triple porch—and wondered: "Perhaps the fact that I have seen no photograph of this doorway somewhat assists this impression." (p. 106) He wanted photographs of cathedrals to be larger, to show more details in the shadows, and to be more like the color of the stone. Many photographers were working to achieve these things in and soon after 1855. The article on Amiens shows that, as Ray Watkinson remarked to me in a recent letter (August 30, 1996), Morris "is a very penetrating observer, and observes himself observing too, which most do not."

Morris's engagement with photography was part of his fascination with all visual forms and properties. In an 1855 letter Morris wrote of coveting an impression of Dürer's print of Saint Hubert. He "very nearly bought it but couldn't afford it, the same being six guineas; I think I should have done so though if I wasn't in hope of getting a photograph of it; the photographs represent the engravings much better than I thought they did, looking very much like impressions whose paper is yellow by age, only somewhat darker. . . ." (*The Collected Letters of William Morris*, ed. Norman Kelvin, vol. 1 1848–1880, Princeton University Press, pp. 13–14) This is an accurate description of the pleasing color cast of a fine albumen print from the mid 1850s. Morris went on to use photography in executing stained glass and tapestries, probably from the 1870s. One of the most impressive exhibits in the V&A show was a full-size tapestry cartoon by Burne-Jones: it had been photographically enlarged by Hollyer from a small design, with touches of color added later by the painter.

Frederick Hollyer (1837–1933) joined the Photographic Society of Great Britain in 1865 and opened a studio at 9 Pembroke Square, Kensington, four years later. He worked regularly with Burne-Jones from about 1870. He made some now-famous photographs of the Morris and Burne-Jones families in the garden of the Grange, the Burne-Jones house in Ful-

Frederick Hollyer, *The Morris and Burne-Jones Families*, 1874

ham. (Sutnik published a fine series of interiors of the Grange made in 1887.) He sold fabulous platinum copies of the works of contemporary artists including G. F. Watts, D. G. Rossetti, and, principally, Burne-Jones. Some of these are touched with color by the artist and can be hard to distinguish from actual paintings. He reserved each Monday in the studio for portraiture and sold his own portraits at the same price as his copies of portraits by painters and draftsman. His best-known Morris portraits were taken in 1884. He was elected to the Linked Ring, the circle of art photographers, which included F. H. Evans, in 1892. Hollyer was described in *The Studio* in August 1896 as "a sturdy, broad-shouldered, good-humored and good-looking man of middle age, who comes nearer to the definition of artist-photographer than any other man in England." His remarks on the art of photography, in the same article, concentrate on its quality as a craft: "In other arts, and especially the subsidiary, it is their very limitations which the craftsmen turn with instinctive

Frederick H. Evans, *Untitled* (through a window in the Tapestry Room, Kelmscott Manor), 1896

recognition to their own advantage. If this principle were only to be recognized and honestly lived up to by photographers in general, we should have results which would be better art, because they would be better photographs." On another occasion he sounded a Morrisian note by saying "it would be a most useful thing, even from the business point of view, if every photographer would resolve that for every negative made for profit there should be another made for love." His own fresh, uncluttered, inventive, and always unretouched portraits bear witness to his belief that "the best professional photographers could do some of the finest amateur work" and that "the one thing needful for photographers, if they are ever to take a position as artists, is general culture, which includes the work of artists of all other classes." He must have taken imaginary portraits constantly: "The photographer who has met a man half a dozen times should know with absolute certainty what is the most characteristic pose and lighting for the face." (The last four quotations are from Harker, *The Linked Ring*, p. 153.) Late in life Hollyer assembled three chintz-covered albums of his finest portraits for his daughter. Eleanor Hollyer gave them to the V&A in 1938, thus providing us with an unrivaled view of the artistic elite of late-Victorian and Edwardian England.

The bookseller and photographer Frederick H. Evans (1853–1943), another member of the Linked Ring, also absorbed a broad general culture and benefited from the values of the larger Arts and Crafts Movement inspired by Morris. In *Frederick H. Evans: Selected Texts and Bibliography* (1992), Anne Hammond suggested sources for the inspiration and title of Evans's best-known photograph, *Wells Chapter House: The Sea of Steps*, including lines from Morris's story "A Dream of John Ball" (1892). Morris described a glimpse of the

Frederick H. Evans, *Untitled* (corner of Tapestry Room, Kelmscott Manor), 1896

interior of a newly built fourteenth-century church: "The white shafts of the shining pavement in the moonlight as though out of a sea." It appears that Evans projected his lantern slides of Wells for Morris at Kelmscott Manor in 1895. Evans returned in the following year to photograph the Oxfordshire house. Morris's ideal of the English country, Fiona MacCarthy wrote, "was the minor English landscape of gray houses in green meadows. His quest took him inevitably to the upper reaches of the Thames. Here he came upon Kelmscott Manor, a beautiful, decorous but by no means little gray stone building in the flat fields southeast of Lechlade. He recognized it with certainty, just as the heroes in his stories recognize their lovers." It was Morris's country home from 1871 until his death.

Morris wrote about Kelmscott in the November 1895 issue of *The Quest*, a copy of which Evans owned. He emphasized the beauty of the attics: "i.e. the open roof under the slates, a very sturdy collar beam, roof of elm often unsquared; it is most curiously divided under most of the smaller gables into little chambers . . . the bigger space is open . . . and has charming views east, west and north." Perhaps Morris himself showed Evans around. He recommended that Evans photograph the thirteenth-century Cistercian barn at nearby Great Cokkeswell. (Two prints are in the J. Paul Getty Museum.) In any case, Morris's words were part of the inspiration with which Evans photographed both the attic and the view. Evans was already deeply dyed in Morris's imagery, as his writings and the contents of his library show. Hammond also tells us that the sale of the photographer's library in 1919 included "A remarkable set of first editions of William Morris," and that Evans retained until his death a number of Kelmscott Press books signed by Morris.

Late in life Morris remarked to Edward Carpenter, the social reformer: "I have spent, I know, a vast amount of time designing furniture and wallpapers, carpets and curtains; but after all I am inclined to think that that sort of thing is mostly rubbish, and I would prefer for my part to live with the plainest white-washed walls and wooden chairs and tables." Evans's Kelmscott photographs capture Morris's characteristically stunning virtuosity of pattern and texture and that final simplicity. The series has the atmosphere of an elegy. Morris died on October 1, 1896. A special issue of *The Artist* was published on October 12, in which Morris was remembered by Aymer Vallance. His essay was illustrated by a portrait of Morris by Frederick Hollyer, by designs of *Ministering Angels* and *Praising Angels* by Edward Burne-Jones and John Henry Dearle and by five of the Kelmscott photographs by Evans. All of these artists were profoundly inspired by the man Vallance described: "Poet, artist, printer, Socialist—he was all these; but how inadequate the words seem to express the completeness, the amazing vastness of his work in every [one] of the four capacities. He was simply prodigious."

WILLIAM S. BURROUGHS AT THE LOS ANGELES COUNTY MUSEUM OF ART: PARIAH OR POPE?

by Frederick Kaufman

"Ports of Entry" traveling exhibition, Los Angeles County Museum of Art, Los Angeles, Summer 1996

In terms of the gallery space allotted to "Ports of Entry: William S. Burroughs and the Arts," this exhibit is modest. In terms of mental space, I have rarely seen a more ambitious show. These five rooms are overwhelming. If anything, this exhibit is *too* exhaustive. Thus does "Ports of Entry" earn the dubious distinction of proving that curatorial triumphs do not necessarily translate into transcendent museum going.

Robert Sobieszek, the museum's curator of photography, deserves tremendous kudos for bringing together these first editions of the novels, this wide-ranging selection of films and audiotapes, the numerous paintings, photographs, sculptures, mixed media, pictographs, and hieroglyphs. Sobieszek even went so far as to track down a bona fide Brion Gysin Dreamachine—a perforated spinning cylinder that supposedly stimulates mental imagery.

Gysin, the Swiss-born surrealist who deeply influenced Burroughs's development as a visual artist, created this device with the misapprehension that it would make him millions. To put it bluntly, he was wrong. Here it is a somewhat forlorn presence, with its tinny Joujouka sound track and earnest warning to epileptics.

This exhibit showcases a number of different Burroughs: The writer, the painter, the photographer, the pseudoscientist, the muse. But all arguments regarding the genre to which the art of Burroughs properly belongs miss the point. Burroughs is, above all, a conjurer, a magician, an occultist intent on breaking the sacred vessels of normative perception. Even at his most unsavory and downright ugliest, there's a redemptive effort behind every sublimation of his conscience, an effort to undo the cultural spell with which we've all been hypnotized. Burroughs is a postmodern Merlin, the possessor of a frightening power to quash quotidian taxonomies, and to co-opt all aesthetic genres for his own, apocalyptic ends.

The sign posted outside "Ports of Entry" bears the following sinister warning: "Viewer and parental discretion is advised." Indeed, this is a powerful and disturbing show. Burroughs sought to transform images into nonnarrative visual mantras, mystical glyphs as a violent antidote to technocratic tyranny. And there is a real edginess to much of the work, from the stark photomontage *William Vacates Rooms* to the haunting painted palimpsest of *For the Angel of Death Spread His Wings*.

The images from his early scrapbooks retain a mysterious, hieratic power. And those homunculi that haunt the late work, such as 1992's *Alien Penetration*, are horrifying yet sinuously beautiful, evidence to the fact that Burroughs's art has neither deteriorated nor retreated in its maturity.

Here are his shotgun paintings, violent and visionary, psychedelic and primitive. Here is Burroughs's voice, his icy, deadpan descriptions of violent orgasm and terminal drug psychosis. Here are his homoerotic underminings of *Time* magazine, his homemade Rorschach inkblots with their visceral, hellish buzz of imminent danger—and then there is that Herb Ritts portrait, made expressly for The Gap.

David Wojnarowicz, *Bill Burroughs' Recurring Dream*, 1978

The presence of a Gap ad in a Burroughs exhibit should give us pause, as should the merchandising effort which includes not only the standard poster and catalog, but a T-shirt, a video, an assortment of postcards, a Burroughs paper-clip box, pencils stamped with Burroughs quotes, and something called Poetry Slam: The Magnetic Word Game—for 2 to 4 players, ages 8 to adult.

All this is somewhat distasteful, but the commercial deployment of Burroughs into popular culture is not an issue because of some arbitrary insistence on rigid distinctions between high and low art; it is an issue because of the responsibility of a museum to present an authentic portrayal of an artist. One of the profound cultural legacies of Burroughs is his own particular brand of cosmic paranoia, a paranoia particularly obsessed with all manner of commodification. To commodify Burroughs is, on this basic level, to strip him of his meaning.

If Burroughs can be bought and sold on a mass level, he himself has become a part of what he has on numerous occasions called the "image sickness," that virus he has gone to such great lengths to deplore in all manner of media. This is not to put on blinders and deny Burroughs's own complicity in the broad-based process that has transformed him into what Gus Van Sant calls "The Elvis of Letters." Yet, if art can be no more than a nuanced advertisement for the self, how can Burroughs ever transcend his popular identity as a wisecracking, black-hatted, counterculture boilerplate?

Clearly, the people at LACMA believe that Burroughs is something more than that guy in the black suit in those Nike ads. Of course, the articulation of this something takes effort. But Sobieszek doesn't even give it a college try, and his pedantic catalog does nothing to address this glaring irony.

Here, Sobieszek's grandiose prose traces Burroughs's influence not only to the likes of John Giorno and Laurie Anderson but also to the graphic layout of *Wired* magazine, the video game "Mortal Kombat," and Bill Gates's software interface Windows 95. Sobieszek is not content to call Burroughs a pioneer. He must also be an astronaut, a freedom fighter, a satirist on a par with Jonathan Swift. He is Coleridge's mariner, Twain's Huck Finn, Castenada's Don Juan. He is Hieronymous Bosch, the Marquis de Sade, David Bowie, Michel Foucault, and Ralph Waldo Emerson all rolled into one.

William S. Burroughs, *Untitled* (Plan Drug Addiction), from *The Third Man*, ca. 1965

And then there is that pretentious indexed listing of cultural studies resources in the back of the book, implying that in order to really understand Burroughs one must also have mastered Barthes's *Elements of Semiology*, not to mention Deleuze and Guattari's *Anti-Oedipus: Capitalism and Schizophrenia*. This miasma of reference comes off as nothing more than sycophantic aggrandizement.

A far more serious problem is that Robert Sobieszek, for all his obsessive didacticism, has not organized this show as well as he might have. Robert Mapplethorpe's beatific portrait is lessened by being placed above a selection of Burroughs album covers. David Wojnarowicz's haunting *Bill Burroughs' Recurring Dream* could have benefited from a curatorial presence to help explicate the Mayan codex and centipede imagery. Yet all of a sudden, Sobieszek is nowhere to be found.

By the end, the show, like an addict's body, has overdosed on its own rush of artistic influence. Its veins have clogged, its eyes lost their focus. The fact of influence—not its explanation—has been sufficient for Sobieszek. The result is an exhibit with impressive horizontal range, but absolutely no depth.

CONTRIBUTORS

VICTOR ANANT has written about India as a foreign correspondent for British newspapers for many years. His varied, wide-traveling journalistic career has included working for *The Daily Telegraph*, *Guardian*, UNESCO (in Africa), and the *International Press Institute* as an editorial consultant throughout Asia. He was the first jazz critic of *The Guardian*. After his years working at the UN, he resigned to devote himself to a historical fiction project, *The Raj Quintet*. The first volume, *Sacred Crow*, has just been published by Penguin India.

MARK HAWORTH-BOOTH is the curator of photographs at the Victoria and Albert Museum. He is preparing his next book *An Independent Art: Collecting Photography at the Victoria and Albert Museum, 1856–1996*, to be published in the fall of 1997; a companion traveling exhibition will open this year at the Victoria and Albert Museum.

FREDERICK KAUFMAN is a novelist, journalist, and critic. A frequent contributor to *Aperture*, Kaufman has studied and written about Beat culture for many years.

MUKUL KESAVAN teaches history at the Jamia Millia Islamia, a university in Delhi. His novel, *Looking Through Glass*, was published by Farrar, Straus and Giroux in 1995.

MYRIAM WEISANG MISRACH, born in France, has written extensively about American culture for such publications as *Mother Jones*, *Outside*, and *Parenting*. With her husband, Richard Misrach, she coauthored the award-winning book *Bravo 20: The Bombing of the American West* (Johns Hopkins University Press, 1990). She has spent many years traveling with Richard. One of the first dates he took her on was to the dead animal pit.

CREDITS

PHOTOGRAPHS: Unless otherwise noted, all photographs are courtesy of, and copyright by, the artists: pp. 2–3: Lynn Davis, Palmyra, Syria, 1995, photograph by Roberta Nieman; Doug and Mike Starn, 1996; Raghu Rai photograph by Gurinder Oswan; Lise Sarfati with Aza in Plochade, Moscow, ca. 1995; Mary Ellen Mark and Jesse Damm, 1994, photograph by Grant Delin; Duane Michals, 1995; Richard Misrach atop Lone Rock I, Bravo 20 Bombing Range, November 6, 1986, photograph by Dr. Richard Bargen; pp. 4–13: courtesy Houk Friedman Gallery, New York; pp. 14–17: courtesy PaceWildensteinMacGill, New York; pp. 18–19: courtesy Leo Castelli Gallery, New York; pp. 24–33: courtesy Magnum Photos, Inc., New York; pp. 52–61: courtesy Sidney Janis Gallery, New York; pp. 62–71: courtesy Curt Marcus Gallery, New York and Robert Mann Gallery, New York; p. 73: courtesy Magnum Photos, New York; p. 74 left: The Royal Photographic Society, Bath, RPS H14 820; p. 74 right: courtesy Victoria and Albert Museum, London, gift of Dr. R. Steele; p. 75: courtesy Philadelphia Museum of Art, Philadelphia, gift of Frederick H. Evans; p. 76 left: courtesy Victoria and Albert Museum, London; p. 76 middle: courtesy The Royal Photographic Society, Bath, RPS 15813; p. 76 right: courtesy The Pierpont Morgan Library, New York, PML 77311; p. 77: courtesy the Estate of David Wojnarowicz and PPOW, New York; p. 78: courtesy Los Angeles County Museum of Art, Los Angeles, purchased with funds provided by the Hiro Yamagata Foundation.

TEXT: p. 6: excerpt from *Hard Travel to Sacred Places*, by Rudolph Wurlitzer, Boston and London: Shambhala Publications, Inc., 1995, pages 60–62; p. 6: "I've fallen in love with the slowness of time," by Ayrev Davis, from *Last Poems*, copyright © 1994 Lynn Davis Wurlitzer and Rudy Wurlitzer.

ILLUMINATIONS FROM DUKE

Caroline Vaughan

BORROWED TIME
Photographs
by Caroline Vaughan
Caroline Vaughan
Foreword by Reynolds Price

"Devastating and quietly revealing. There is something both equalizing and transforming that takes place when a subject is placed in Vaughan's lens. She has a way of evoking and capturing a moment of intense self-recognition in her subjects."—Alex Harris

112 pages,
66 b&w photographs,
paper $24.95,
library cloth edition $69.95

ILLUMINATIONS
Women Writing on Photography from the 1850s to the Present
Liz Heron and Val Williams, editors

544 pages, paper $24.95,
library cloth edition $69.95

Duke University Press
Box 90660
Durham, NC 27708-0660
http://www.duke.edu/web/dupress

SOME STUFF NEVER WEARS OUT.

There's something special about a product that's built to last. At Chimera, we've dedicated ourselves to years of research in materials, improvements in design, and a unceasing dedication to craftsmanship and consistency. From our specially developed fabrics to our durable Speed Rings and flex poles, Chimera Lightbanks are designed to provide you with pure, controllable soft light for years to come. A product that you can reach for time and time again . . . just like your favorite pair of boots. Please call for our catalog and the name of your nearest Chimera dealer. 1-800-424-4075. Built in Boulder, Colorado, U.S.A.

C H I M E R A

An Innovative Program
leading to a

MASTERY OF FINE ARTS

Degree

With concentrations in:
Photography
Digital Imaging
Film & Cinema
Arts Administration
Creative Writing
Arts Administration

World-famous faculty
Design your own program
Low residency requirements

For 24 years, Photography's Leading Workshops Center

Write, call, fax or e-mail us for a catalogue.

The Maine Photographic
WORKSHOPS
2 Central Street · PO Box 200
Rockport, ME 04856
Phone: 207-236-8581 · Fax: 207-236-2558
E-Mail: MEWorkshop@aol.com
Internet Web Page: http://www.MEWorkshops.com

EDWARD WESTON:
HIS LIFE AND PHOTOGRAPHS

Illustrated Biography
by Ben Maddow
Afterword by Cole Weston

This rare Aperture classic documents the achievement of a pioneer whose work during the first half of the twentieth century changed the course of photography. *Never to be reprinted,* the book contains 158 exquisite reproductions, each the same size as the original print.

197 black-and-white photographs, 13" x 12"
300 pages, hardcover, ISBN: 0-89381-043-6, $175

Nude Floating, 1939

accompanied *by Edward Weston Portraits*

Nude floating, 1939 is a luminous portrait of Weston's second wife and greatest model Charis Wilson. This limited edition black-and-white print is made from the original Edward Weston negative, printed and signed by his son, Cole Weston.

250 numbered copies and 20 artist's proofs. 8" x 10". $950/ea for editions #1-75.

TO ORDER CALL
1-800-929-2323